D0794987

THE MANY FACES OF MEN

Dr Stephen Whitehead is a Senior Lecturer in
Education and Sociology at Keele University,
Staffordshire. He is a member of the UK government
Cabinet Office Forum on Gender Research and
lives in Lancashire with his wife, Suwanna.

The
Many Faces
of Men

THE DEFINITIVE GUIDE
TO THE MALE SPECIES

Stephen Whitehead

arrow books

Published by Arrow Books in 2004

3 5 7 9 10 8 6 4

Copyright © Stephen Whitehead 2004

Stephen Whitehead has asserted his right under the Copyright, Designs
and Patents Act, 1988, to be identified as the author of this work

Arrow Books Limited
The Random House Group Limited
20 Vauxhall Bridge Road, London, SW1V 2SA

Random House Australia (Pty) Limited
20 Alfred Street, Milsons Point, Sydney,
New South Wales 2061, Australia

Random House New Zealand Limited
18 Poland Road, Glenfield
Auckland 10, New Zealand

Random House South Africa (Pty) Limited
Endulini, 5a Jubilee Road, Parktown 2193, South Africa

The Random House Group Limited Reg. No. 954009

www.randomhouse.co.uk

A CIP catalogue record for this book is available from the British Library

Visit www.stephen-whitehead.com for Stephen's biography,
list of publications and details of his gender and relationship guidance services.

ISBN 0 09 946635 X

Typeset by Roger Walker

The Random House Group Limited supports The Forest Stewardship
Council® (FSC®), the leading international forest-certification organisation.
Our books carrying the FSC label are printed on FSC®-certified paper.
FSC is the only forest-certification scheme supported by the leading
environmental organisations, including Greenpeace. Our
paper procurement policy can be found at
www.randomhouse.co.uk/environment

Printed and bound in Great Britain by Clays Ltd, St Ives plc

For Su

Contents

FOREWORD

From the moment of our birth we are learning masculinity and femininity, and we do it amazingly fast. Usually, by the time we are three years old we have picked up many of the key gender signals that will stay with us, in some form or another, for the rest of our lives. Gender is not something we are born with. It is something we learn. Society and culture tell us how to behave as men and women, not our DNA. Gender is different from sex.

As an academic who has studied and written about masculinity for fifteen years, my research having taken me all over the world, I am constantly surprised by the many different types of men there are. It is a fascinating subject. Contemporary research into men and maleness tells us that masculinity is fluid, changing, while culturally and historically specific and, importantly, multiple. There is not just one type of masculinity out there, but many.

This book came about as an attempt to pin down the different patterns of behaviour that underlie the contemporary male species. It's based on a mixture of the latest academic research, my own work in sociological theory, interviews with women – naturally the best experts on men – and a lifetime of personal observation.

I hope that by reading through these faces you will come to a better understanding of the differences within the male species, how masculinity works, how men come to experience and act out male behaviour, and where it comes from. More importantly, I hope you enjoy the book and get some amusement from spotting which male faces are present in your life, or maybe which male face you are. Take it as seriously or as lightly as you wish, but I can guarantee you will never look at men in the same light again.

Stephen Whitehead

ACKNOWLEDGEMENTS

Many thanks to all at Random House connected with this book, especially Lindsay Davies, Anna Cherrett, Charlotte Bush and Jo Wheatley. My appreciation to my agent, Amanda Preston, for her valued guidance and support, and to Amelia Cummins and Vanessa Forbes also of Sheil Land Associates. My thanks to work colleagues, Carol Hough and Melanie Broad, who commented on an early draft manuscript. Lastly, I am especially grateful to En Hudson for unwittingly providing me with the inspiration and to all those men who have, intentionally or otherwise, revealed to me their faces.

UNDERSTANDING MEN

You may think you know all there is to know about men, but do you? Do you really know who they are, these men who father us, love us, live with us, lead us, work with us and for us? Is it true, as many women have suggested to me, that there is just one type of man – predatory and unreliable? Or are there two types – the 'good boys' and the 'bad boys'? What do different types of men really think about sex, love and relationships? Which men make the best lovers? Which men are dangerous to love? Which men are the empire builders? Which men are the followers? The aim of *The Many Faces of Men* is to provide answers to these intriguing questions

Men are subjected to much more questioning now than in the past. Over the last decade the spotlight has been turned on them, exposing the characteristics of masculinity in a way that has never happened before. We no longer believe all the stereotypes. We know it's much more complicated than that. So this book is not about differences between men and women – that's old news. It's about the differences between men.

In a way, it's a self-help book for women to recognise what sort of man they are dating, have dated or are about to date. With it, you will be able to tell the bad apples from the good, to spot the stronger men among the weaker ones, to separate the serial seducers from the marrying types – no more complaints of betrayal by weak and pathetic men who say one thing and do another. Rather than stumble through endless unsatisfying relationships, you can get an idea of what a particular man is like, not just on the surface but deep down. Checklist your date's characteristics against the descriptions in the book. Take the book to work and look at the men around you in a new light.

Flirting with a man by email is one of the joys of technology, but it is also fraught with risks. Now you can ask just the right questions to find out about his inner self, possibly getting a better idea of his character than he has himself. For those already in relationships, this book can be a ready resource from which to predict your boyfriend's behaviour – and his possibilities as a long-term lover or husband.

Use it to check which men make the best husbands, friends, lovers, fathers and partners. You will discover why sport, booze and work are such comfort blankets for many males, and which men are most attracted to younger women. It tells you which types of men prefer to spend time with their mates rather than their loved one. It warns women which men are dangerous, and yet why they are often the most irresistible. It shows how to recognise different types of men, live with them, work with them – and avoid them. In revealing the many faces of men, this book signposts the reader through the maze that is masculinity.

At the same time, it will help men to understand their own character better, which type of masculinity they have and the consequences this has for them and the women in their lives. They will see, possibly for the first time ever, their strengths and weaknesses described in frank and candid detail and will never look upon their masculinity in quite the same light again.

The forest of men

One of the problems when trying to understand men and their behaviour is that we can easily get caught up in all the stereotypes, although we know they confuse rather than enlighten. The variety can be lost in simple explanations and generalisations. For example, we might see a gang of youths out on the pull on a weekend, but look more closely at those males and you'll see a group of quite different characters. Some are there for the sex game, some for the booze, some because there's nothing good on television and some are there because they just like being with their mates – they'd follow them anywhere. Already, by the time they get to their teens, you can spot the leaders and the followers, the emergent Alpha Males and the Zebedees. This is not engrained from birth, but by the time the average male reaches his teens, his masculine character is pretty well formed. He's on his way, but with all of life's little surprises to navigate on his journey towards adulthood.

It is precisely because men are everywhere that often we don't see the individual. Instead, we see merely a forest of men – 'trees' that all look alike. The forest may be pretty difficult to miss – men have a lot of physical presence, they are usually the first to be heard and they generally still control the worlds of work – but this forest is full of different types that we tend not to notice.

Despite the fact that they are all around us and despite the millions of words written by and about them over the centuries, men still have the capacity to surprise. The most contradictory of creatures, men can appear brave and committed one minute, yet hesitant and insecure the next. They can be macho with their pals, but timid in front of their mothers. They can love their children deeply yet rarely hug and kiss them. They can travel the world looking for that special someone and when they find her they can be up and off again within months. They can kiss their mates on the football field but never in the pub. They can love a woman with a ferocious passion yet still be unfaithful to her. Men's masculinity can appear rock solid, yet it is as easily burst as any balloon. Every woman who has ever loved a man has opened the Pandora's box containing masculinity and sexuality. One minute she's sensitively massaging a bruised male ego, the next she's an audience for her man as he postures and swaggers in front of his mates. What heterosexual woman hasn't, at some point, asked herself, 'Can I trust my man?' She will have agonised over whether he really loves her, whether his heart belongs to her alone. She will have thought, 'Can I change him?' And later on, she will have reflected, 'Do I want to change him – is it really worth the effort?' If you are facing these dilemmas, reading this book will help you to decide if it really is worth the effort, and, if so, what sort of man you want him to turn into.

Is it all down to nature or nurture?

Many people believe that men's actions and characteristics can be explained biologically by hormones, genes and DNA, but if that were the case, we could reduce all men down to maybe one or two types. Is it that simple? I would argue not. Detailing numerous male types reveals the diversity of men and their characters, but more than that, it shows how men are presented with models of masculinity and then spend much of their time and energy trying to imitate them. In order to appreciate the importance of what is happening here, you have to stop thinking of masculinity as something men are born with, and start seeing it as a model or as a role that they have to perform if they are to be accepted as males.

Most psychologists and sociologists recognise that environment plays the major part in determining who we are. Men's masculinity is not hard wired into them at birth. The brains we are born with are not the brains we have in adulthood. Like our bodies, our brains grow and develop. They acquire connections according to what happens during childhood and throughout our life. To understand men, you have first to understand that it is nurture, not nature, that rules their lives. Masculinity is not something men are born with but something they aspire to.

Can men change or will they stay one type all their lives?

If you think a man you know particularly well is a mix of faces, something between, say, a Uniform Man and a Zebedee, that's entirely possible, although it also suggests he might be in transition. It's clear that many men do shift between faces during the course of their lives. For example, I have come across a man who was a typical Adonis in his twenties, muscular, tattooed, obsessed with looking good, but through a number of key incidents and influences on his life he started to change. He's now in his mid-thirties and is an emerging Libman, doing a part-time degree in psychology and much more reflective and cerebral than before in his work, life and relationship. He still has the tattoos to remind him and his partner of that other face, but he doesn't spend time at the gym any more and it's quite possible to see Libman emerging, and strongly. It's very common to see men make transitions connected with age and maturity. For instance, a twenty-something Cool Poser may turn into a high flying Alpha Male in his forties, while many of us have seen examples of the transformation of staid Corporate Men into Manchild once they hit the big five O.

However, while some men change there are many who seem reluctant to alter their behaviour and attitudes. Some male types are receptive to change and some are not, some are hopeless cases and some are worth working on. Some will always try to avoid intimacy, and fear emotional expression, while others, such as Teddy Bear, have that most valued and useful attribute, especially in relationships – emotional intelligence. Murdoch will always be an empire builder while Libman is happy to be a househusband. The calculating, manipulative types who use romance as a seductive ploy will probably remain that way, as will those who are sincere in their love lives.

What makes different men change is never easy to predict. It is often what British sociologist Anthony Giddens describes as the 'fateful moments' occurring in their lives. We're all suscep-tible to these profound, life-changing incidents. For example, your man might change with the birth of a son or daughter, he might change if he loses his job or wins the lottery, he might change if he falls in love or suffers the loss of a dearly loved one. Over the course of a lifetime, it is possible for men to change, even if they don't mean to and don't realise it themselves. Some men will be Uniform Man in their twenties, transforming into Wayne in their forties or fifties.

Many of these male types have younger versions. For exam-ple, some young men may be attracted to the idea of being such a macho type of guy as Rottweiler but their youth and inexperi-ence mean they don't really fit the bill completely, they don't fully measure up. So what we often see on the streets are a lot of teenaged wannabe Rottweilers. They may become the fully fledged versions in ten or so years' time.

Some male types are more fashionable than others within certain age groups. You are more likely, for example, to meet a twenty-something Gadgetman than a sixty-something one, whereas Manchild is, by definition, a much older male, probably in his late forties or fifties.

The variations are particularly apparent in the modern age. For example, just look at photos of American men attending baseball matches or going to work in the early twentieth cen-tury, or black and white film of British football matches in the 1920s and 1930s. The massed ranks of working-class males in

New York, Chicago, Leeds or Manchester show how similar men were then. They all wore the same clothes, the same hats, talked the same language, drank the same beer, did the same sorts of jobs, and then went home to wives who cooked their dinners – not any more. This uniformity has all but disappeared to be replaced by diversity and difference.

A further point to note is that no man ever reaches a final state of masculinity. He is always working at it, trying to be a man in whatever setting he finds himself. Observe men in bars, in all-male groups or at sporting events. They may look like they are just there with their pals, but what they are also doing is practising being a man, trying to get it just right, ensuring they give off the right male signals, speak the right male language. Most men have to police their behaviour, avoiding doing anything that jeopardises their fragile sense of maleness or throws their masculinity into question – especially in front of other men. Some men are so insecure they can only really feel confident through membership of male-dominated clubs. Men such as Club Man, Neanderthal and Uniform Man really feel confident only when surrounded by like-minded males.

Which are the most desirable types of men?

Precisely how sexual desire and attraction works for each individual is impossible to explain. It's certainly not just about looks. Every man and woman, if they wish to, and regardless of size and shape, can make himself and herself appear attractive to members of the opposite sex. It's not just about age – increasing numbers of men and women in their sixties and seventies have active sex lives today. Is it about money and material wealth – the notion that women's desire for men is a search for security? Do women just want a man who is wealthy and has a big car? Is it that simple? Many men still believe this to be so, which is one reason why they are happy to show off their Rolexes, black BMWs and designer clothes. For many men, especially those such as Murdoch, acquiring wealth has a lot to do with phallic posturing – their subconscious tells them there is some link between the size of their bank balance and the size of their penises or their sexual potency.

But in an age when women are ever more financially independent, money counts for less in the romance stakes. Today, many women don't need a man for financial security. They want something much more important – love and emotional support. However, while most women accept this as a given, many men find it very difficult to understand this basic dimension of contemporary relationships. They still stumble into relationships with women, thinking that their traditional views and ideas are somehow 'manly' and attractive. For the most part, they are very wrong. Today, women are more likely to be attracted to 'switched on males', those who can be sensitive and manly, passive and powerful, certain and yet, at times, insecure.

Some men are much better at this than others. While some types of men would rather die than admit to weakness or emotion, those such as Libman or Teddy Bear are okay revealing their softer sides. It is ironic that the men displaying heavy masculinity are often those most needy in relationships. They are the ones who need the most care and attention from their partner. They are not that strong after all. It's just a performance, one that many women come to see as pretty unconvincing.

Much research into love and desire suggests that many women tend to go for those men who satisfy some deep psychological need. The men they fall in love with may nourish some inner hunger for acceptance by a dominant male – maybe an older, more experienced man. Certainly, most women do like experience in a man for it signals and reinforces their own maturity and desirability – also older men are more likely to be appreciative of, and able to accommodate, a mature woman's unique character and needs. At a more complex level, an older male lover might represent a paternalistic figure, maybe an absent or distant father. Yet women can also be attracted to younger, apparently more virile and fit young men. Maybe younger women select mates solely on the basis of who they'd prefer to father their children. If so, increasing numbers of women are using this as a very temporary connection, preferring to raise their children single-handed rather than remain in an emotionally sterile relationship after the passion has died.

Research also indicates that large numbers of women are attracted to those men who are dangerous – the risky lovers. Such men as Cool Poser and Romancer represent a real challenge for many women. They think to themselves, 'Maybe I can be the one who settles this man down, maybe I alone have the power to seduce him and keep him.' Before you embark on such a quest, read this book. It will tell you which men it is worth seducing with permanent love in mind, and which men to seduce for temporary fun and laughs.

Often there is no clear rationale or reason behind love or sexual desire. They have a habit of creeping up on us, surprising us with their intensity, disturbing us out of our smooth running, otherwise predictable, lives. We often get ambushed by sex and love.

Sexual desire is not just about one type of man suiting a particular type of woman. For one thing, as we get older, more experienced, so our tastes change. This is one of the dilemmas of the modern age – we're starting our sexual lives much younger and living much longer. Boys and girls growing up in the twenty-first century can expect to enjoy sexual careers spanning sixty years or more. The idea that we will be sexually happy and emotionally satisfied with just one individual, or even one type of individual, throughout our active lives just doesn't hold true any more. In fact, the average span of heterosexual relationships is now just over three years, which tells us that more and more men and women are playing a much looser, less long-term, game of love and romance.

Men may have been experimenting and having multiple or serial relationships for a long time, but the same is now also true of women. As recent research shows, women today are much more sexually active than women of previous generations. Now a woman can be predatory and single-minded in pursuit of the opposite sex when she wants to be. She can also be quite indifferent to men. She doesn't need any man to take care of her. She is her own woman and any man who comes into her life must be prepared to recognise this and accommodate her individuality and desire for independence. By the time she reaches her late twenties, the typical modern woman will have had numerous relationships and sexual encounters. She will have sampled many of the men in this list. But which of these types will she most desire? Who will she want to settle down with?

It's impossible to answer these questions for every woman, but in describing each male type I have tried to list their main attractions as well as those characteristics that women are likely to find least attractive. For example, many women may well fall for the intense intelligence of Preacher, but become tired of his political posturing. A woman may swoon with delight at Adonis's sculptured body, though he prefers his own curves to hers, or she may come to realise that there is much comfort to be had in the quiet, reliable, but rather boring predictability of living with and loving a Trainspotter or Wallflower.

Whatever their different preferences in men, one thing most modern women are now seeking in love and relationships is a level of emotional maturity in their partners. They are less inclined to shoulder all the emotional labour required in a relationship, and they are most unlikely to remain with a man who is physically and emotionally violent to them. Women have more choices open to them in this modern age and one of the choices they are making is not to get involved with those men who are unable to give them democratic love. Modern woman may well decide that a brief sexual encounter with, say, Neanderthal is what they need, physically, at a particular moment in their lives, but they are unlikely to take on such a man as a lifetime commitment.

Can you change men?

The idea that women can change their man has a long history, too long to explore in this book. Yet how easy is it for women to change the man in their life? Is it possible? Is it even to be recommended?

Among the main influences on all of us, men and women, are the loves in our lives. Any woman should recognise that she has the power to change the man she loves, but if you are contemplating taking this path, be careful because it does carry risks. Think about these three things before starting out.

Firstly, do you know who your man is now? Are you absolutely clear what his strengths and weaknesses are? This book will help you establish what type of man you have in your life, or men for that matter. Once you know that, at least you will know what your starting point is, though your end point may be much more difficult to determine.

Secondly, you must be clear what your aim is and what price you are prepared to pay to achieve it. I do know of a woman who changed her man from a Wallflower into a Corporate Man. I also know of others who helped their men become Alpha Males or aided their Murdoch to build his empire, but this takes a lot of effort and determination. Have some idea of whom you are trying to change your man into. If you manage to settle down

Backpacker, for instance, be clear that you want him to be, say, a Libman, rather than a Wallflower or Zebedee.

Thirdly, do you know what type of woman you are? If you understand your strengths and weaknesses, you will be in a much stronger position to decide what type of man will complement your own characteristics. We are seeing more and more women aspiring to become Alpha Female. Can two Alphas live together in quiet harmony and peace? That's another book.

Where is the perfect man?

During the course of writing this book, I gave various drafts to women friends of mine to read and comment on. One comment I invariably got back was, 'Well, after all this research you've done on men, where is the perfect man? What is he like?' While I fully appreciate why many women are interested to see if the 'perfect man' actually exists, this comment troubled me because it suggested that most of the twenty-seven faces were not that likeable. This may be true in some cases, but each type has his strengths and weaknesses, each type has positive and negative characteristics. Like most other aspects of life and the human condition, everything is in the eye of the beholder. After all, even Attila the Hun and Hitler were loved by someone.

So rather than trawl through these pages looking for a 'perfect man', try to see these faces as complex and deep, contradictory in places and often insecure, for this is much closer to the truth. You may find some of these types boring, abhorrent or repellent; you may find some attractive, fascinating, enchanting and sexy. But that's men for you. It's their differences that are most interesting, not their similarities. Indeed, I would argue that there are more differences between men today than there were, say, fifty years ago, and the more the world becomes a global village, the more those differences between men seem to exist across, not within, cultural spaces. For example, we can no longer assume that English men are somehow innately different from Spanish men, or that Italian men are inevitably more romantic and passionate than, say, German men. It's increasingly the case that it's individual men who are different, not the cultures they inhabit.

How to use this book

Each face has been given a name that reflects the essence of the masculinity being described, whether it be Rottweiler, Achilles or Zebedee. Brief notes of the guy's main characteristics are followed by a detailed description of what he's like. A number of important questions are answered individually – can he be trusted in love, how romantic is he, is he the marrying kind, what sort of woman does he go for, what is he like as a father, as a boss, as a friend and is he the man for you? I have called upon contemporary sociological and psychoanalytical theory in compiling the list of faces and include a brief, succinct insert on this with each face, for those who are interested. In summing up, it's down to the nitty gritty with a few more, important questions – how do you spot him, how does he perform in the bedroom, what if he's already your partner? Finally, there's a key, telling question for you, and sometimes for him. If you know a man who is that face, you might test the question on him and see how he responds.

Whether male or female, straight, bi, or gay, happily married or looking for love, I hope you find *The Many Faces of Men* revealing and interesting. Moreover, I hope you agree with me that all twenty-seven faces neatly capture that elusive thing called men.

THE TWENTY-SEVEN FACES OF MEN

ACHILLES

Main characteristics

Very attractive but deep character; unsettled and troubled; gifted but flawed; confident but needy.

What's he like?

In ancient Greek mythology there was one male hero who stood out among all others. He had everything – charm, strength, beauty, grace and valour – and he was invulnerable. He could not be beaten or struck down but he did have one small flaw, one weak spot – his heel. And so, in Homer's *Iliad*, Achilles' heel proved to be his ultimate downfall. There are men around today who are just like Achilles. They seem so strong and powerful, yet beneath that grace and assurance they carry an air of tragedy, always promising much but never quite fulfilling it, caught as they are by a single fatal flaw. This is Achilles. This man may indeed look like a god. He may be handsome, sophisticated, charming, but watch out. His life is not all it seems – there are hidden, murky depths. Women sense this man's vulnerability, their antennae picking up his underlying weakness, and that can be so attractive. Here is a man who needs saving from himself, and many women want to rise to this challenge.

If Achilles sounds like a man you'd want to get to know better, remember that he's likely to be a mature man rather than a teenager. He's been around, experienced life, travelled and had some success in his chosen career. Life has not been all bad to Achilles, far from it. He's enjoyed much that life has to offer, sensually, materially and emotionally. So what's his problem? His problem is that somewhere along life's tortuous route he faced a difficulty or traumatic incident that he was not able to overcome. He faced it but, crucially, never faced it down. This incident, whatever it might have been, cut him deep and now he has to live with the fact that he is not so special after all. He has to accept the reality of this particular vulnerable aspect of his personality. Importantly, he has had to face the fact that he is just like everyone else – less than perfect.

Although this incident in his life was so disconcerting for Achilles, don't expect him to reveal it to you. It is layered much too deep in his persona. In fact, many Achilles don't even admit their own weakness to themselves – that can be much too threatening. Instead, they go through life presenting themselves as one of the 'lucky few', performing like confident leading actors on the Broadway stage, their secret anxieties left in the dressing room. It's no coincidence that many Achilles are actors and musicians. Show business is one of their natural habitats along with politics.

Can Achilles be trusted in love?

Well, in one important way, yes he can. Unlike, say, Romancer, most Achilles are not serial shaggers or compulsive seducers, though in some cases their secret weakness does have strong sexual dimensions. Achilles may well come to hurt those who love him, but it is not intentional. Achilles doesn't get off on hurting others. He is not a deliberate hurter. He is genuinely likeable and usually reliable in love, but he is much deeper than he appears. Achilles is a bit like the Indian Ocean – warm inviting waters at the surface but the deeper you go, the colder and darker it gets.

What you cannot expect from Achilles is a sign round his neck saying 'Be Wary of Me'. That realisation comes later, when you know him better, but don't be surprised if, meanwhile, you tumble into love with this man. He is that rare beast – both a woman's man and a man's man. He demonstrates a real comfort with his feminine side, and at the same time can play the masculine role with his mates with ease. He likes the company of men and yet he gets on very well with women. He is very good at presenting himself in social situations as a 'good bloke', a friendly, gregarious, social animal. Articulate, considerate and concerned about other people's feelings, Achilles won't let you down when you take him home to meet mum and dad, nor will he embarrass you when you introduce him to your female friends. He won't flirt with your best friend behind your back – though she might like him to!– and he won't deliberately set out to emotionally abuse you.

Is Achilles romantic?

Things happen around Achilles, not least because his relaxed and confident manner encourages others to befriend and support him. Life with him is invariably full and fulfilling. He is not a man for boring routine and slippers by the fireside. As far as romance is concerned, Achilles is one of the best male faces to love. Much of his life is an attempt to cover up and conceal his vulnerability and make amends for those moments when his flaw gets the better of him, and because of that Achilles tends to go for the more lavish expressions of love and passion. Not for him a weekend away in Whitby, dining on fish and chips, or a few nights in Des Moines, Iowa, frequenting Pete's All-Nite Diner. Achilles likes the best and he will want to share it with you. So expect the unexpected – weekends in Vienna visiting the opera and browsing the fashionable boulevards, for instance; or maybe he'll unexpectedly pick you up from the office early one Friday afternoon and fly you down to the Rio Grande to lie under the Milky Way, counting stars, listening to just your two hearts beating and the haunting call of night owls. Beneath that blanket of stars, it will occur to you that he is just like a star himself, a star whose sheer radiance and gravitational power pulls other planets, other beings, towards him. You will feel this power and marvel at his luminous energy, yet even as you begin to succumb to his charms and yield to your desire, so something in you whispers 'be careful'.

Is Achilles the marrying kind?

Yes he is. For Achilles, marriage or partnership is more than a commitment to love and cherish a woman. It is a very important anchor in his life, the focal point of his stability – and stability is something he has learned to value very much. In fact, he yearns for it. He is astute enough to recognise that he is not complete without a partner who loves him and, importantly, knows and accepts his weakness. Achilles' flaw may be his propensity to love too much, beyond reason and perspective. It may be that he has an addictive personality. Drug or drink problems often surface with this character. He may have an unresolved fear of being rejected in love, having been traumatised by the loss of a loved one or parent at a tender age. Perhaps he's gone through a very difficult divorce and feels immense unresolved guilt at having left his children, or not having access to his children. He may have a compulsive personality that constantly gets him into difficult situations – financially or emotionally. Whatever his weakness, Achilles can live with it much better if he has a woman who loves him and understands him, and he won't let go of that sort of love easily. As his partner and soulmate in life, you are the means through which he can appear complete and worthy, not least to himself.

What sort of woman does Achilles go for?

This is a tricky question to answer. Much depends on where Achilles is in his life when you meet him. For instance, that crucial moment when he has just experienced the traumatic event that forced him to face his vulnerability can be a difficult time for any partner of his. You'll need fortitude, commitment and a lot of patience. Remember, he's going through a storm and changing as a result. He won't be the same man after this incident. You may walk away at that point, saddened but sure that he's not for you, or you may well come to be the one who helps him pick up the pieces. If you are the one to 'rescue him', then know that he needs you badly – though don't necessarily expect him to acknowledge it, at least not at first.

Achilles needs a woman who is resolute and resourceful, someone who is stronger than he but doesn't feel the need to keep reminding him of it. His ideal woman will be as much if not more interesting on the inside than on the surface. Shallowness and superficial beauty are not for him. She will have to be able and prepared to roll with the blows of life for the sake of love. Although he may appear so on the surface, Achilles is not the sort of bloke who wants a woman to adorn his ego; he needs much more than that. He needs someone who will forgive him his weakness and who will tell him it's okay when that weakness gets the better of him. Importantly, as he comes out of his crisis and into the world once more, he needs you to be a key supporting player in his own production starring himself.

What is Achilles like as a father?

Achilles is usually one of the more enlightened men when it comes to doing his share of the housework and childcare. In that respect, his is quite a modern masculinity. However, children of Achilles find themselves torn between loving their father's strengths and hating his weakness. Their teenage years can often be fraught with angst as they come to recognise their otherwise god-like father is not so god-like after all. Once they come to accept who he is and start seeing him in a more realistic light, their relationship with their dad can be excellent. Achilles' own recognition that no one is perfect makes him a potentially excellent father and once those difficult teenage years have passed, he can be a very good friend to his kids.

Could you work for Achilles?

As a boss, Achilles has the capacity to generate loyalty and affection among his staff. This is partly because they usually see only the best of him, not the flaw. If, however, Achilles' flaw does manifest itself in the work environment, it can all come undone very quickly and his staff can feel betrayed as they come to realise the man they respected and admired is not so perfect after all. Most Achilles are astute enough to ensure this doesn't happen and, in general, this is one of the better male faces to work for.

Would you like Achilles as a friend?

Achilles doesn't seek perfection in others, even though he has struggled to find it in himself. This fact alone makes him a potentially interesting, loyal and thoughtful friend. Be careful about getting too close to him if you sense that there are aspects of his personality that could be damaging to you. Mostly this won't be the case, but this guy runs very deep and friendships can be early casualties if he comes to grief on his own particular rocks. At moments of crisis in his life he suddenly won't be around any more. He'll be in retreat – from everybody, but mostly himself.

Scientifically speaking

Whatever it was, the 'fateful moment' or critical incident in Achilles' life had profound personal consequences for him. As philosopher Jean-Paul Sartre might put it, Achilles experienced profound existential disruption, rendering him very insecure about himself both as an individual and as a man. To that point in his life, Achilles had never really looked over the edge and into the abyss of self-awareness spreading out beneath him. The experience was shattering. Sure, he moved on from it but life was never quite the same again for him. He was mortal after all, and human. From then on, much of his life has been spent attempting to manage the realisation of his mortality.

Is Achilles the man for you?

Although he may sound like a bit of a challenge, Achilles does have many good points. He may have an inherent weakness, but once you know what it is at least you are in a position to deal with it and to accept him, flaw and all. Of course, whether or not he can be deemed a 'good catch' depends on just what his flaw is, but most Achilles are not dangerous to know. They are just a little dangerous to love, at least for those women who are not alert to the darker side. One thing to be aware of is that Achilles knows he is attractive, often to both women and men, so his ego is not that small. He can have a slightly arrogant air, appearing a little too confident and sure of himself at times. He is used to admiring glances and friendly smiles. He is not used to rejection, although he has experienced it. Achilles lives in a world where he is more often than not the centre of attention and it's something he carries with aplomb; indeed, it is something he has come to expect. In seeking out, encouraging and surrounding himself with such adoration, Achilles is able to conceal his flaw, but to love him you have to go beyond this performance to the very core of the man. You have to know him better than he knows himself.

To sum up

Achilles is a man who could be truly special, unique even, and yes, invulnerable if only he could overcome his single flaw. Are you the woman who is up to this challenge? Think carefully before you take the plunge. Whatever the flaw is, he can hide it well. On the surface he may appear to be a man with it all, a man who has little to fear from life, but beneath this attractive exterior troubled waters stir. Don't get in without a lifejacket.

HOW TO SPOT AN ACHILLES

This man is very difficult to identify but a giveaway is his image – most Achilles are smooth and polished men. They like to keep it this way because they know it is the best means of concealing their flaw. What you see is not necessarily what you get.

HOW DOES ACHILLES PERFORM IN THE BEDROOM?

Quite a sexual animal, this one. Will particularly enjoy sex in risky situations and places, such as lifts, trains, outdoors, the office. Think of Bill Clinton.

WHAT IF ACHILLES IS YOUR PARTNER?

If you are living with Achilles, it's most unlikely that you haven't discovered his weakness. You need to find out to what extent he's able and prepared to acknowledge and open up about it. Talking between loved ones is always the best way to deal with it, the essential first step to managing the problem.

MOST LIKELY TO SAY

'Perfection is only in the eye of the beholder.'

KEY QUESTION

Achilles asks you to marry him. Do you draw up a pre-nuptial agreement or rely on fate and the bumpy road of love?
Answer: If you love him, and know his flaw, say yes, but with your eyes fully open.

ADONIS

Main characteristics

Obsessed with his body; likes to be near mirrors; takes lots of vitamin supplements; usually sports a fake tan; has smooth firm gluteus maximus.

What's he like?

As most women know, the male body can be a beautiful thing – shapely, firm and pulsating with strength and energy. Yet many men allow their bodies to develop in an almost haphazard manner, depositories for alcohol, nicotine, dope, e-numbers and animal fats. It is as if their bodies don't belong to them. They just occupy them for the time they're on earth and if they work, fine, if they don't, too bad. However, not all men are like this. There is a type of man who sees his body as a shrine, and he worships at it virtually every day. Such a man is Adonis. It's not that Adonis is obsessed with appearing perfect, like Achilles is, although he is very self-regarding. He's not that bothered whether people think him an intellectual giant or not, or gravitate towards him at parties. He cares less about his clothes than his muscle tone, and his hair is usually cropped short simply so it doesn't interfere with his hundreds of daily press-ups. No, Adonis is a man like all others, but unlike many men he gets to feel manly by exhibiting raw, exaggerated manliness in his physical presence, in his bulging biceps and swollen chest muscles glistening with sweat. His countless hours of gym work, and maybe the steroids, have built a body that is, for him, the epitome of masculinity. In a very male way he is quite beautiful, sculptured as he is like a Spartan warrior, rippling with testosterone.

I once observed an Adonis on a beach in Southern Thailand. He was with his wife and two young children. They arrived midmorning to find themselves a spot shaded by the coconut trees but within striking distance of the azure blue sea. The beach was not crowded but there was that constant movement of sun strollers up and down. While his wife settled down in the shade and his two children played in the surf, Adonis just stood there, hands on hips, chest out, stomach rippling, legs astride, looking and watching. He was not that young, probably early forties – his lined face and neck gave his age away – but he was impressively muscled and he knew it. His posture and pose were relaxed but he was there to display himself to others, men and women. His shorts were brief and every now and again he'd tuck them up even tighter in order to expose more of his finely tuned leg muscles – and his groin. It was quite impressive really, the dedication to display that he showed. He never moved far from that position, just the occasional walk around, down to the water's edge to see the kids were okay, the odd word with his wife and then back to the business of manly exhibition. This went on for several hours and right through the intense midday sun. A typical Adonis doing what he does best – showing off his body.

Can Adonis be trusted in love?

You might imagine that a guy like Adonis would be pushing all that iron in order to attract women, but is this so? In fact, what Adonis really yearns for is the admiring gaze. That is what the

Adonis on the beach was doing – inviting others, both men and women, to gaze upon him and admire. He was not doing it in order to pull women. So while it's important to recognise that Adonis is fundamentally a vain character, don't imagine that this makes him a dangerous man to love. Most Adonises should make steady and reliable partners. They get a strong sense of identity from the pursuit of physical perfection in themselves, not from achieving sexual conquest over others. In short, Adonis's exercise schedule is not for his benefit – in a very profound way those countless hours of pushing weights are for you and me.

Is Adonis romantic?

What happens if you find yourself gazing on Adonis and wanting to find out a little more about him? What sort of partner is he likely to make? Well, love and romance have to be learned. They don't come with user manuals, especially in the complex modern age, so it's unfortunate for Adonis – and any potential partner – that while he spends so much time working out, his time for actual contact with the female species becomes limited. He may know the difference between lactic acid build-up and aerobic capacity, but his knowledge of women is much less developed. This is not one of your more sophisticated seducer types of men. With Adonis, what you see is very much what you get. He may be complex but he's not got the depth of, say, Chameleman, nor is he a very reflective guy. He really is a one-dimensional man, at least on the surface. You'll get to know what makes him tick pretty quickly, but finding out what else lurks beneath the tan can take longer. Is it worth it? Probably. Once you get beyond his obsession with his physique, and if you can wean him off his addiction to pushing weights six days a week (even Adonis needs a rest day), you've probably got yourself a reliable, honest type of bloke. His approach to romance is likely to be rather traditional and limited and his understanding of women will similarly be rooted in stereotypes and traditional values, but despite all this he is genuine. Don't expect him to be a smooth operator in social situations, and be patient with him in posh restaurants – he's likely to struggle to tell the difference between a Chardonnay and a Claret. But what the heck, there's more to life than fine wine.

Is Adonis the marrying kind?

Yes, you have a good chance of getting this male type to the altar or settling down with him in a long-term relationship. Make sure you arrange the honeymoon to fit in with his training schedule – the hotel should have a fitness centre and pool, and, ideally, a nice beach where he can display his muscles and tan. Another tip if you marry Adonis, he's really into supplementary diet foods, so it's most likely you and he will be dining on high carbohydrate and high protein foods much of the time. Don't expect to be eating TV dinners.

What sort of woman does Adonis go for?

Adonis will usually look for a woman who complements his simplistic physical sense of masculinity. She will ideally be keen on fitness and exercise herself, or at the very least be interested enough in working out to want to pound the treadmill occasionally. Expect Adonis to be much more interested in the appearance of his partner than in her hidden, arguably much more interesting, depths.

One woman I spoke to told me that she and her friends referred to these types of blokes as 'sunbed queens', not a very flattering description for men they considered a little sad and socially limited, obsessed with 'looking good' but never quite managing to look 'hip'. The hardened, dark-tanned look that comes from too many hours under the fluorescent light of the sunbed is a real giveaway, made worse if Adonis chooses to adorn his chest with a gold medallion. Yet Adonis's sense of masculinity really is, for him, encapsulated in his body and for this reason it's important that he shows it off to best effect. This man is not one of your boutique squirrels – he doesn't buy and hoard the latest fashionable gear. He much prefers the T-shirt and tight jeans look, with perhaps a leather jacket to set it all off – minimum gear for what he considers to be maximum effect.

What is Adonis like as a father?

Not very imaginative and likely to be less than useful when it comes to changing nappies but, think of all those hunky photos you can take of Adonis posing semi-naked with the baby in his arms. At least he will appear the epitome of modern masculinity, even if he's really a throwback to a more traditional age.

Could you work for Adonis?

As you'd expect, Adonis makes the perfect boss of any gym or fitness centre. This is his natural environment. He's also excellent as a personal fitness coach, although his own high standards can be a bit hard to meet. Don't work for him if your idea of exercise is a walk down to the pizza parlour or burger bar.

Would you like Adonis as a friend?

Yes, just so long as you share his obsession with keeping fit and the body beautiful. If this is the case, you can expect Adonis to be a reliable friend, honest and up-front. He's not one to play mind games although he can be quite competitive when it comes to comparing physiques. If you are a more cerebral type, he's likely to bore you pretty quickly.

Scientifically speaking

Adonis's body is the vehicle by which he comes to feel and act as a man. He relishes other people gazing at him because, for him, it confirms his masculinity. According to one philosopher, Georg Hegel, this is a subconscious process we all experience – an obsession with our biological self. However, among the male faces, only Adonis invests his very sense of identity in his physique.

Is Adonis the man for you?

It's quite likely you have already met Adonis, in which case you may well have made up your mind whether he's the man for you or not. His vanity and obsession with pushing weights may put you off but, as Madonna discovered, there is, of course, one benefit from dating Adonis – you get your own, very personal, fitness coach. Quite apart from the fact that many, if not most, women do love the feel of nicely toned male muscle around them, his knowledge of physical exercise can come in very handy. With Adonis you have someone to chivvy you into that early morning jog or joining the local gym. He'll be there to encourage you when your pounding heart wants to give out, or the pain in your quads from all those squat thrusts reaches agony level. Sure, he'll have high expectations of what can be achieved on the exercise mat, but despite this, and whether you want to be something of a female version of him or merely feel the need to lose a few pounds and tone up the rest, there's no better type of man to be with. Today twenty press-ups, tomorrow twenty-five, next week forty, he'll have your exercise schedule worked out in no time and he'll absolutely love and admire you for following every sweaty minute of it. Importantly, he'll be by your side while you do it. A further advantage with this type of man is that if there is an Adonis you fancy, the easy bit is getting his attention. All you have to do is pop down to his gym and ask him if he's available as a personal fitness coach. But beware – love him, adore him, caress him, but never forget that, ultimately, Adonis likes his body much better than yours.

To sum up

Adonis is not one of your more complex male faces. He gets his sense of masculinity simply from feeling and looking good. His idea of 'handsome' leans more towards Arnold Schwarzenegger than it does Tom Cruise, so expect him to be a little rugged, both in his approach to love and romance, and in his looks.

HOW TO SPOT AN ADONIS

Easy – just look for the man bulging out of his suit or T-shirt and sporting an all-over tan. It is important not to confuse Adonis with the real thing, by which I mean those men who devote their lives to a sport that demands maximum physical fitness. Adonis's ideal environment is the gym, not the track or field and not the football pitch. He doesn't build muscle tone in order to throw further or kick harder; he builds it in order to feel good about himself as a man. Don't expect to see Adonis in the London Marathon, although you may get the odd one competing in a local charity jog.

HOW DOES ADONIS PERFORM IN THE BEDROOM?

Average. It would help to have plenty of full-length mirrors around so that he can see himself in action.

WHAT IF ADONIS IS YOUR PARTNER?

I'm sure you'll be in pretty good condition yourself. Adonis is not keen on women who don't reflect, in their own feminine physique, his ethos of the body beautiful.

MOST LIKELY TO SAY

'My hamstrings are playing up again.'

KEY QUESTION

Does his gym have women members?
Answer: If it does, sign up yourself – you've always said that one day you'd start regular exercise. If it's an all-male gym, perhaps you should look elsewhere. After all, quite a lot of Adonises do actually prefer the gaze of men.

Alpha Male

Main characteristics

Extremely competitive animal; mostly reliable in love; likes to be the leader of the gang; preoccupied with work; the next deal is the reason he's alive.

What's he like?

Some people are born leaders and some have leadership thrust upon them, or so Alpha Male believes. But whether nature or nurture is the reason he's the way he is doesn't matter to Alpha Male because there is only one place he is going to be, and that is at the top of the heap, leading the pack, the first in line. Life is a rat race and he is the lead rat.

Margaret Thatcher famously said she was 'not for turning', in the process giving her supporters and enemies alike a clear indication of the strength of her unbridled self-belief and willpower. She was self-evidently an Alpha Female, and the male version is no different. He is strong, determined, resolute, resourceful and very capable. He can also be ruthless in the pursuit of his aims. But don't get the impression that this man is just about self-aggrandisement; that would be much too shallow an aim for him. Sure, he will purr in quiet pleasure when his deeds are spoken of in awe late at night in the city wine bar or by the 18th tee of his exclusive golf club, but seeking such recognition from his fellows is not what drives him. He is extremely accomplished, socially skilled and highly intelligent. If you believe in the inevitability of the cream always rising to the top in any society, Alpha Male is the living embodiment of that Darwinian theory. In short, he fervently believes he should be at the top of the heap.

Alpha Males come in every shape and size and every possible skin colour, but they are usually attired in suits. Why suits? Well, it's the suits who run business, politics, commerce and bureaucracies, and it is most likely that Alpha Male will surface in one or more of these arenas. This is no angst-driven artist or tweedy, bookish academic we have here. Your typical Alpha Male is more likely to be spotted pursuing a career in the civil service, aiming to be a senior Whitehall mandarin. He could be in politics, with a picture of No. 10 Downing Street hanging in his office to remind him of his ultimate destination, or he could be a senior manager for Proctor & Gamble, already well established on the organisational ladder and heading towards Chief Executive of an overseas division.

However, not all Alpha Males choose to go into corporate life or run their own businesses. Many find that professional sport is their forte. So if he's not in a suit, you may well find Alpha Male in shorts and T-shirt, pounding out the miles on an athletics track or doing heavy duty circuit training in a gym. A common characteristic of Alpha Male is his unbending competitiveness. This is one man who must win at everything he attempts. These Alpha Males don't go into tennis, basketball or marathon running for the exercise – they are seeking confirmation that they are the best. In that respect, the sporting Alpha Male is no different from his namesake in politics or business – he's just fitter.

Can Alpha Male be trusted in love?

Despite the fact that Alpha Male puts more effort into his work than his relationships, love is very important to him. He relishes the stability of a permanent relationship and he's unlikely to be serially unfaithful, although that doesn't mean he won't be tempted. It's also important to note that while Alpha Male has set views and an unreflective character, he is one of the more analytical of male types and learns quickly in whatever situation he finds himself. So if you fall in love with him, don't make the mistake of underestimating him. This man understands the meaning of emotional intelligence, but it's not for him. In his view, emotion and sensitivity are for followers, not for leaders of men such as he is. Alpha Male's ambition will get him into many scrapes, but he has the ability and inner strength to bounce back from adversity. Indeed, this sophisticated, clever and articulate male type only really comes alive when he is fighting his corner, competing, in charge, at the centre of things, with all eyes on him, preferably looking up to him. For this reason if for no other, work is his defining environment. All else comes second, including his relationships.

Is Alpha Male romantic?

In understanding the role of romance and passion in Alpha Male's life it is important to remember that from a relatively early age he has been very clear about what he wants. From his early teens he has had a sense of destiny, a feeling of being a little different. This doesn't always make him nice to know or especially easy to work for, not least because he is very prone to arrogance and he doesn't suffer fools gladly, but it can make him very attractive to women. His certainty and intelligence are real turn-ons for many women, and this, coupled with the fact that he is clearly going places, means Alpha Male is not a bad catch in the marriage stakes. But you have to get in early. Unlike Manchild, he is not the sort of man who will be looking back in his late sixties at several marriages and an equal number of divorces. The typical Alpha Male is very much a one-woman man. He may find his soulmate while at university, or she may appear one sunny summer afternoon at the family home, a friend of his sister. Wherever he meets her, once he's decided she's the one, he will pursue her with all the awesome determination he can muster. Expect no quarter if you are the one being chased. Alpha Male can do romance as well as most other men, but possibly without the deep emotional engagement of, say, Teddy Bear. However, when it comes to red roses, tender loving cards, unexpected gifts, surprise trips to Paris, Alpha Male is your man.

Is Alpha Male the marrying kind?

Most of his masculine identity comes from successes at the office, so Alpha Male tends to place less emphasis on his home life than some other types do. For Alpha Male, there is a clear distinction between home and work, and it's the latter where he gets his kicks. But don't mistake this attitude for indifference towards his family. Far from being indifferent, Alpha Male can be a loyal, loving husband. Unlike Backpacker, he's not the type to roam and he's not after the serial sexual escapades that drive Romancer. What we have with Alpha Male is a man who knows the meaning and value of security, which is why he tends to work in large, secure organisations and why he prefers marriage to the looseness of bachelordom.

Married life gives Alpha Male many advantages in his pursuit of his aims. Firstly, on a practical level, it means he has a clean, warm and inviting home to return to after his game playing in the corporate jungle. Secondly, he can be a devoted father, secure in the knowledge that his wife will do most if not all the child-work – the kids' nursery is unlikely to have Alpha Male's mobile phone number while they will certainly have his wife's. Thirdly, Alpha Male is astute enough to know that every corporate leader needs a good wife alongside him, both as a practical and an emotional support.

What sort of woman does Alpha Male go for?

This guy's perfect partner is someone who complements his self-image, but not in any tarty or glitzy way. He likes a down-to-earth woman, someone with lots of common sense and maternal instinct, but who can also look tantalisingly glamorous when the occasion calls. Alpha Male's soulmate will have to be prepared to put her own career on hold in order to support his. Don't forget, this male face is heading for the top of the career ladder so he'll be looking for a wife who'll be resilient enough to follow him to whatever part of the globe he might be posted by his organisation.

What is Alpha Male like as a father?

Great – when he's around. The rest of the time, which is most of his life, he's likely to be a hands-off dad. Avoid getting into big arguments about this. He'll just see you as being selfish and ungrateful for all the breadwinner stuff he's into. In his eyes, he's taking care of his family through all his hard graft down at the office. He fails to see that there is more to parenting than this, and as a result, he may retire on an excellent pension but he will, sadly, hardly know his now adult children.

Could you work for Alpha Male?

Although Alpha Male is not an ego-driven empire builder such as Murdoch, he does have many of those characteristics, especially in his capacity for hard work combined with a quicksilver brain and impressive single-mindedness. The big differences between these two faces are, firstly, that Murdoch makes rules rather than follows them, whereas Alpha Male is more of a rules man, which is why he does best in organisational settings. Secondly, while Murdoch is always something of a loner, doing his own thing, Alpha Male can prosper and flourish in any team – so long as he leads it. He considers team working to be fine as an organisational theory but he's not so keen on it in practice unless he's in charge – though he'd never admit it to his underlings. In other words, as Alpha Male sees it, team workers are the organisational infantry while leaders are the one's who have the drive and the vision. Such views may seem to fly in the face of modern cultural democracy, but Alpha Male is too pragmatic and in too much of a hurry to start worrying about the equity of it all. For Alpha Male, life is a Darwinian-inspired meritocracy and only the best and most able deserve to rise.

Would you like Alpha Male as a friend?

Despite his generally good social skills, this male face does not set out to cultivate friendships. He's very similar to Murdoch in so much as there is a calculating side to his character and in whom he seeks to befriend. Also, he can be devastatingly candid, so be warned about that! However, if you are close to him, you can expect him to be loyal and constant. He'll disappear from your life for months if not years on end, and then suddenly reappear when he's managed to free up a little time, away from all that organisational game playing.

Scientifically speaking

In his obsessive pursuit of getting to the top, Alpha Male exhibits all the characteristics of what Australian sociologist Bob Connell terms 'hegemonic masculinity' – that is, a dominant, powerful way of being male that is largely respected by other males, even if they don't all replicate it. Alpha Male is usually quite highly regarded by other men, even if they don't necessarily like him. They accept his position at the top and would only challenge him if they wished to usurp him. In other words, the biggest threat to Alpha Male's position usually comes from other Alpha Males, or from rarer faces such as a Murdoch or a Chameleman. It's interesting to note that with women now increasingly replicating male behaviour, we are seeing more Alpha Females challenging their male counterparts.

Is Alpha Male the man for you?

If you fancy being Alpha Male's soulmate, know that his love for you comes at a price. He'll expect you to look up to him. He doesn't want to be in competition with you for a position on the Board of Directors. He'll expect you to put your career second and to be, first and foremost, a reliable, devoted wife and mother. He'll expect you to be skilled at organising those occasional Friday night dinners for especially invited colleagues, and at innocently flirting with his boss while you serve the crème brulée. In return, you will get the Harrods charge card with which to ensure you are impeccably turned out at all times. And of course, you'll get to drive the Range Rover.

But don't expect it to continue like this throughout your married life. Remember, he wants you, he loves you and, most importantly, he needs you but, as he sees it, you are not the reason why he's here on earth. As time moves on and Alpha

Male becomes ever more embroiled in the organisational politics of his multinational corporate employer, so he will appear more distant, more preoccupied, more self-obsessed. His diary will be full to overflowing, just the way he likes it, and as a CEO, he will now have a personal assistant to keep it all on the rails.

To sum up

Marry Alpha Male for the material benefits and security that will come from association with him rather than for his undivided attention. Sure, he'll remember the roses on your birthday but only because his PA has it in her diary. He can delegate, he can take charge, he can control, but his real skill is in making his wife, secretary, underling, feel special, even when what really drives him is his upward movement on the career ladder.

HOW TO SPOT AN ALPHA MALE

Whether he's in his Italian silk suit or his Adidas sweatshirt, Alpha Male gives off all the signals of being obsessed with his work. Look for a man who can talk of little else other than his ambitions. He has no hobbies.

HOW DOES ALPHA MALE PERFORM IN THE BEDROOM?

He has potential but you need to get him to switch off first. Don't allow him to bring his mobile phone into the bedroom.

WHAT IF ALPHA MALE IS YOUR PARTNER?

Congratulations – mostly. He may have a tendency to manage you at times, just like he manages his staff, but at least you're unlikely ever to be poor. Nevertheless, try to keep an eye on those store-card limits.

MOST LIKELY TO SAY

'If you can't stand the heat...'

KEY QUESTION

Ask Alpha Male to write down your birth date and those of his children. Then ask him to write down the current share price of his firm. Which of these numbers is he most likely to remember? *Answer:* It's the share price, I'm afraid. The only numbers he's guaranteed to carry in his mind are his company's latest profit and loss figures.

BACKPACKER

Main characteristics

A man travelling light; sexy but dangerous; relationship day-tripper; loving but uncommitted; his bags are always packed.

What's he like?

Some men are harder to love than others. With some of these male faces you may need to be Joan of Arc, Mother Theresa and Marilyn Monroe all rolled into one. With others, it doesn't matter who you are, you will still have a hard time pinning them down. Perhaps the hardest men to cope with are those who are very easy to love but very difficult to hold on to. Achilles and Sigmund may have their complex sides, but at least they are unlikely to roam far.

This is not the case with Backpacker. It's not so much that he sets out to be dangerous to women; it's just that he is like one of those exotic butterflies in the Amazon rainforest – so attractive and interesting you just wish he'd settle down long enough for you to pop him in a box and take him home. But he never stops flitting from flower to flower. The second you stop to look closer, so he is gone.

Backpacker's fatal attraction is that he has an air about him that tells you he is fascinating to know, honest, trustworthy and, yes, good in bed. But never forget that while all men have strengths, they also each have weaknesses. Even Teddy Bear, one of the nicest male faces, can be just a little too nice at times – and nice doesn't always make for sexual chemistry. What we have with Backpacker is someone who can be charming but also sufficiently mysterious, and naughty, to get you hooked – and keep you interested. He's not a user of women, he doesn't play mind games with you, and he won't try to oppress or damage your emotional state. He is a genuine guy, confident with women, with few hang-ups about sex and even fewer desires to dominate.

So what's Backpacker's problem? He is an habitual relationship traveller. He always has his bags packed and he always has one eye on the door. Backpacker is one of life's perpetual tourists or day-trippers – he never commits, he never settles down, he is always just arriving or just about to go.

Can Backpacker be trusted in love?

Absolutely not! Nevertheless, despite all the warning signals he gives off, most women who've got something of a sexual career behind them will have fallen for a Backpacker at some time in their lives. They'll have gone for his cool, worldly charm. They'll have been impressed by his knowledge of life, politics, philosophy, religion. They'll have listened in admiration while he recounted his experiences of hiking over the Atlas Mountains of Morocco. They'll have secretly marvelled at the self-confidence that enabled him to hitch a yacht trip down to Biarritz. There is not much Backpacker hasn't done, and not many places he hasn't been to. He may be a little reticent recounting some of his past relationships, and you'll come to wonder why he's never found the one woman for him, but despite these little warning whispers in your head, the feeling that this man is the one for you just won't go away.

At first, you cannot believe your luck, to have found such an interesting worldly-wise guy. After all those less than fascinating experiences with Neanderthal and Zebedee, after devoting your precious time and energy to the ego of Cool Poser, here, at last, is a man who is your intellectual equal – a man who knows his own mind, seems uncannily good at reading yours, and can find g-spots even you didn't know you had. His very presence in your life boosts your self-belief and hope in love.

Best of all, he seems to value you, want you, need you. He listens when you talk, remembers what you've said, and doesn't think he's always right. He treats you with respect in public and with just the right amount of control in bed. Perhaps he even loves you. Certainly, for a time at least, he acts like you are the centre of his whole world. He always answers your calls, he never places unreasonable demands on you, and he looks at you with such intense interest and desire even when all you are doing is recounting your recent shopping trip to Tesco. You start to plan. You allow yourself increasingly to dwell on the exquisite belief that here is the man of your dreams.

Then one day he is no longer there.

Is Backpacker romantic?

Unfortunately, yes, very much so. In some ways, Backpacker can be as damaging to a woman as Romancer or Cool Poser for he is very loving and sincere in his feelings and most women who get close to him will sense this. Few are immune to his charms. Whatever their ages and backgrounds, women can fall for Backpacker in quite a big way. They love his air of independence, his experience, his worldliness, his intellect, his sincerity. Crucially, most are well into the relationship with him before they become alert to his downside. Backpacker may sound like bad news to many women, but to understand him you have to appreciate that he lives his life by one very simple motto – 'Life is a journey and to live it to the full you have to keep travelling the road.'

Is Backpacker the marrying kind?

Only in his twilight years. Your typical Backpacker will have had many careers and many jobs. He's likely to be university educated and will have a high degree of self-confidence. He is adaptable, reflective and intelligent. He really does like and respect women, and if you ever settle him down long enough to set up home with him, you will find that he cleans loos and irons shirts. Despite the emotional rigours that come with continuous relationship travelling, Backpacker does keep going for quite a long time. In fact, it's probably the travelling that keeps him young – he rarely looks, or acts, his age. Expect him to start his journeying while in his early twenties and still to be packing his bags in his fifties. Eventually, the years on the road will take their toll and he will have to settle down. I've come across quite a few older Backpackers chilling out in exotic locations, married to a local woman and to all appearances blissfully happy. The sharp eyes still emit that naughty, knowing sparkle, but they cannot conceal an inner sadness at the realisation that the travelling days are over.

What sort of woman does Backpacker go for?

Backpacker's greatest dislikes are repetition, routine, predictability and habit, so, not surprisingly, he's not out there looking for a woman who prefers the kitchen sink to the departure lounge. Similarly, he has a deep fear of being tied down too long, either physically to one job or place, or emotionally to one woman. He does not seek security, never worries about his pension, and is propelled by a wish to learn, experiment, understand. Some might see him as a bit of a misfit, too involved in pursuing his own agenda, a bit eccentric even. This restless nature of his is not simply a consequence of him being unable to commit to love, and you'd be mistaken if you imagined that in loving women – he doesn't seduce them – all he is doing is adding more notches to his backpack. What drives Backpacker is curiosity. All that travelling, both physically and emotionally, is born of a deep urge and desire to know himself, and the world, better. If you are of an equally restless nature, maybe you could pack your bags together.

What is Backpacker like as a father?

If he sticks around long enough to play the part of dad, Backpacker can be a great parent. He's liberal minded, but firm at the same time. His children, especially as they get older, come to appreciate the fact that he's not judgmental and that his worldly experience might be helpful when they're considering their own adventures during their university gap year. However, only have Backpacker's children if you are able and prepared to be a single parent. Should you cross the Rubicon with Backpacker and have his child, don't rely on Relate or the Child Support Agency to put it right for you. On the other hand, he may not be much good as a daily hands-on father, but he does make an excellent weekends-only dad. His kids are one anchor in his life he doesn't pull up.

Could you work for Backpacker?

Work, for Backpacker, is largely a means to an end. He may be clever and skilled, he may have professional qualifications to his name, but he's not so obsessed with corporate life as many other male faces. Backpacker is not one of your workaholics. If he is your boss, he's likely to be very flexible, perhaps too flexible for his own good. He has little or no interest in organisational politics – something every good boss should have, partly because it protects those under him. You won't find him hard to work for, but maybe a tad frustrating at times because he doesn't take any of it very seriously.

Would you like Backpacker as a friend?

Yes, so long as you can keep up with his rather eccentric lifestyle and, more importantly, you are prepared not to be judgemental about his relationship comings and goings. If you consider yourself to have high moral standards, Backpacker could trouble you. He can, however, be an interesting guy to know and if you can appreciate his mindset, you'll always welcome him turning up unexpectedly at your door.

Scientifically speaking

Backpacker's endless travelling, both emotionally and physically, arises from a deep-rooted quest for himself. The French psychoanalyst Jacques Lacan argued that there is no core entity to the individual, only the elusive pursuit of identity and the desire for it to be understood by others. Most of us achieve some sense of identity through putting down roots and being social animals, but for Backpacker, it comes through the travelling, never the actual arriving.

Is Backpacker the man for you?

If you think that this man might just be worth scrutinising a little more closely, be aware that one of the big attractions for many women who make out with Backpacker, even if they do spot his bags lying half-packed under the bed, is the conviction that they can settle him down. Many really do believe they are the ones to curb his restless spirit. Well, they can try, and they may well find it fun while they do so, but in the end his desire to get on the road again tends to win through. At that point, there is only one thing to do. Don't fall out, don't slam the door, don't hate him, don't be bitter and angry – just let him go. Tell him you'll never forget him and that your door is always open to him – not your heart, because you have to protect yourself from his restless impulses. That way, you'll be more than happy for him to pop by now and again for light refreshments.

To sum up

So is the advice deftly to avoid Backpacker should you spot him heading your way, bags packed from his last love? Yes, if what you are after is one man for the rest of your life. If, however, you feel that just to know this man will be an enriching experience, go for it – but keep one eye on the door at all times. If your Backpacker is young(ish) and giving off all those signals that suggest his restless nature is not entirely curbed, be careful. And if the parting does come, try to part as friends and not as bitter ex-lovers. You will appreciate having such a good and interesting person in your life once all the love stuff has died down. It's good advice to do a bit of backpacking yourself – that is, put it all down to experience.

HOW TO SPOT A BACKPACKER

If he's attractive, experienced, well-travelled, confident – and straight – why isn't he married or with a partner? Ask him about his previous relationships and who did the leaving, him or her. Alternatively, look at his passport.

HOW DOES BACKPACKER PERFORM IN THE BEDROOM?

This one will certainly get your juices running. He knows all the tricks. Enjoy it while it lasts.

WHAT IF BACKPACKER IS YOUR PARTNER?

Well done. How did you accomplish it? Perhaps you've managed to change him into a Corporate Man. If so, I hope he's still an expert with the g-spots.

MOST LIKELY TO SAY

'Sorry, I've a train to catch.'

KEY QUESTION

If you sense you're getting emotionally involved with a Backpacker, how do you protect yourself?
Answer: Take out travel insurance – that is, don't fully commit yourself until he has, if he ever does.

CHAMELEMAN

Main characteristics

Very adaptable; patient and careful; attractive to many eyes; artful; smooth, urbane, but never just the man you think he is.

What's he like?

In the rainforests of the world, one creature above all others is expert at using its environment both as self-protection and in order to prey on other species. Its ability to move and hunt, and yet remain unseen, is legendary. This creature is the chameleon. It frequents both the higher and lower branches of the rainforest, always alert, always watching, and yet hidden to all but the most observant eyes. This species is not exclusive to the jungle; it can be seen in more familiar places, such as a nightclub, the office, the beach, shopping in the supermarket. This human version is Chameleman and he is every bit as skilled at adapting to his immediate background as his animal counterpart. Of all the male types, he is the most accomplished at remodelling himself to merge in with his fellows. He is the most artful at blending into whatever social situation he finds himself in. He is one fascinating character.

There is no doubt at all that you have met Chameleman but whether you spotted him among all the other male faces is another question, unless of course you are married to him. In that case, you may be aware that the man in your life lives in little boxes, little compartments, and that you and the marriage are in one of them. Once you've got over the frustration of his many personality adaptations, you may be at least a little impressed at his expertise in slipping from one social compartment to another. I know compartmentalising is often seen to be a dominant characteristic of men, and this is certainly true of several male faces, but none have mastered this skill like Chameleman. He has it down to a fine art.

Novels and films often use Chameleman as a main character, but to be successful they have to capture his multifaceted personality, the essence of which is to appear bland and ordinary while concealing something much more interesting. Think of Matt Damon's character, Tom Ripley, in the film 'The Talented Mr Ripley' and you'll get what I mean, but don't run away with the idea that all Chamelemen have murderous tendencies. Chameleman is, in appearance, friendly, amenable and not someone you'd look at twice. He could be the department store manager, or the bloke who delivers the mail every morning. He could be serving your drink in the bar, or he could be your local politician.

Can Chameleman be trusted in love?

It would be so easy to say that this is one face you should never trust, and never get close to, but is this really the case? Certainly, from the above description you'd be forgiven for thinking that here is a male face to stay away from, a man you could never fully rely on, and I would agree with you. But then I remind myself of those Chamelemen I've worked with and whom I have genuinely liked. You see, they can be very nice people. They are friendly and sociable and good to have around. They are not prickly. Being nice isn't the same as being trustworthy though, especially when it comes to love, so my advice is to tread carefully. First you have to spot him coming and that is the tricky part with this male face. You should also be aware that many Chamelemen are experts at infidelity. They are accomplished at all the clandestine manoeuvrings that come with pursuing affairs. They get so good at it they become a little addicted to the thrill of it all. This is what makes Chameleman a dangerous lover – he is fundamentally likeable, he can appear so honest and genuine, yet all the time he has other agendas, none of which you will ever fully know.

Is Chameleman romantic?

As you might expect, Chameleman does have very highly developed antennae for spotting likely lovers. I won't call them sexual victims because many women, and gay men, revel in his attention. Once he's set his eye on someone he'll follow up with romantic gestures. Chameleman moves forward slowly but relentlessly. He is cautious but extremely persistent. He knows all the right moves to make and he will flatter you with his gallantry and thoughtfulness. His ways of romance will appear spontaneous, but they are carefully considered. Chameleman can be the epitome of urbanity and casualness, quite a cool character in fact, or he can be more rough and ready, dominant both in and out of the bedroom. He is so many faces, he is all the faces, yet none of them.

Is Chameleman the marrying kind?

Chamelemen can be anything they want, including married and, to all appearances, very settled in their lives. So whether or not a particular Chameleman chooses to live his life as a single man or as a married, domesticated one depends almost entirely on him. He can perch himself anywhere on the social ladder and in any social setting. It's up to him how he uses his talent. For example, I came across one especially fascinating Chameleman who lived out an entirely dual existence for several years. He was married with one child. He had a middle-management job that apparently took him to France and Germany quite frequently. He lived an ordinary life, in an ordinary house and he never drew attention to himself. But he had a dark and deep secret. He had two homes, two partners and two sets of children. When he wasn't living with his legal wife, he was living with his common-law one and, remarkably, neither knew of the other's existence. He moved from one home to the other almost on a weekly basis, hiding his movements behind the apparent demands of his job and his frequent 'travelling abroad'. The homes he'd set up were in different towns, but not that far apart. How he managed to cope with the emotional and physical complexity of it all remains a mystery to me, but he did. It went on like this for nearly ten years until one day he made a mistake and left a clue to his hidden existence in his pocket. His wife found it and everything unravelled very quickly.

I lost track of that particular Chameleman but my guess is he's using his talent to effect elsewhere, perhaps not with two partners, but almost certainly in some capacity that requires him to be different things to different people. Maybe he is now a politician, appearing so reliable, certain and caring to his electors while hiding his real concern, which is to maintain appearances; or perhaps he's chosen to focus his gift for social interaction on office politics. Professional politician or office politician, either environment is comfortable for a Chameleman. Indeed, if you wish to spot this male type, it's a good idea to start looking in these places first. He may be the union leader who somehow manages to climb far up the management ladder, serving two very different masters, playing two very different roles. He may be the social climber who continually pops up at the most exclusive parties, gregarious and welcome, although just who invited him no one is sure. He may be the unnoticed young man in the mail sorting room, who is constantly watching, observing and learning. Come back in ten or so years' time and for sure he won't still be in the post room. Check the executive lounge.

What sort of woman does Chameleman go for?

This depends on whether he's looking for something permanent or casual. If it's the latter then Chameleman will seek out a woman who meets his particular needs at a particular time – docile mistress, quick shag, or someone to help him achieve his career ambitions – his boss's P.A., for example! If he's set his mind on a more lasting and committed relationship then Chameleman's preferred woman is one who doesn't ask too many questions of him, loves him unreservedly, and who, if she does come to realise her husband has more compartments than a high rise condominium, keeps that knowledge to herself.

What is Chameleman like as a father?

Being a father is, for Chameleman, just like any other social role he chooses to take on. He will do it with aplomb and apparent devotion. Like most fathers, he will struggle with the messy bits, such as coping with a child's sleepless nights or tantrums, but he'll invariably come up smiling if a little ragged. Just because he has so many compartments in his life doesn't mean he's not capable of feeling and demonstrating love in several of them. In fact, that's what he does best – showing sincerity to everyone.

Could you work for Chameleman?

There is no doubt that Chamelemen can make good bosses – they know it's in their own interests to be liked by their staff. Your Chameleman boss will give the impression of valuing your views and your work, he will be there for you if you seek his help or advice, and he's most unlikely to be overbearing in management meetings. He will always listen. I guess every organisation needs its share of Chamelemen. They are a necessary part of the fixtures, as essential as the fax and photocopier. They oil the wheels and in times of chaos and crisis, when those such as Zebedee and Trainspotter are careering around confused and unsure, Chameleman will be your anchor – understanding, knowing, confident and still smiling.

But despite his adaptability and intelligence, Chameleman is not immune to danger. All his carefully laid plans and astute compartmentalisation can come to grief if he becomes too confident, too sure, too arrogant – and too careless. I've known some Chamelemen to achieve much in their profession, yet for it all to come crashing down around their heads when they over-reached themselves. Perhaps they seduced just one too many secretaries or office juniors; maybe they misjudged and backed the wrong horse in the organisational power sweepstakes; or, more likely, they tried to back all the horses and got found out.

Would you like Chameleman as a friend?

Chameleman has the ability to social climb with the speed and grace of a leopard climbing a tree. This male face is big on friendships and alliances. He has the gift not only to survive but actually to thrive in most types of organisations. He is rarely short-tempered or brusque, he is always there with a ready smile and he is a superb listener. If he chooses, he can be everybody's friend. Yet despite working with him or having him as a friend for many years, it's unlikely you'll have recognised him as a Chameleman because this is one male face you will never truly know. His manner, language, his very character, can be altered to reflect not just his surroundings, but those he seeks to impress or influence. And whom does he want to impress? Well, this depends on which box he is occupying at a particular time. If it's his sexual box, whom he is out to impress depends entirely on his preferences. Be warned, though. Whether gay or straight, you won't spot him inching towards you until you are well in his sights. Not all Chamelemen are sexual predators, but they do have the ability to notch up scores on the bedpost if they are that way inclined.

Scientifically speaking

In many ways, Chameleman is the archetypal postmodern male. He is never completely himself. He is, as French philosopher Jean Baudrillard might put it, an abstraction or 'simulacrum' – that is, a whole range of symbols and images that individually and together serve to render him whole, at least in his imagination, although all that ambiguity and multiplicity make it difficult. He is fluid, flexible and in a constant state of transformation. It is through this complex process that he achieves some sense of himself as a masculine subject.

Is Chameleman the man for you?

What if you fall in love with this character? Isn't he dangerous to desire? Well, to a great extent this depends on you. If you are a woman, or man, who always sees the best in people, who turns a blind eye to your partner's little misdemeanours, who loves the simple things in life, and who is happy to put your loved one's needs before your own, Chameleman may be your ideal guy. If you are such a nice and straightforward person, you'll make the perfect partner for this highly complex and multifaced character. The two of you would make an excellent match. What's more, he will know this and value it. In fact, he will treasure it and treasure you. Don't pry into his other boxes. Accept what he is to you and how he is to you as the real him. Don't be too soft with him – it's better that he has some boundaries with you – but in the end be prepared to forgive and move on. If you can manage all this, you will have one of the most fascinating male faces in your life. For the most part, he'll be who you want him to be. That will be his gift to you.

To sum up

This is, potentially, one of the few really dangerous male faces. He loves the secret, the clandestine, the hidden. He is an accomplished social animal and quite political when it suits him. It's important to know that he has his own agendas and that you're unlikely to be aware of them. Yet, despite all this, you could live with and love this man without ever feeling betrayed or damaged. He would put you, and the relationship, in one of his boxes, one of his mental compartments, and the two of you could live happily ever after. On the other hand, one day you might accidentally discover he's got several boxes, well hidden, which reveal a very different side to him. Is it worth the risk? Only you can answer that one.

HOW TO SPOT A CHAMELEMAN

Look out for an apparently bland yet sociable character who always manages to be on everyone's Christmas card list.

HOW DOES CHAMELEMAN PERFORM IN THE BEDROOM?

He's excellent at role playing, so if you're into sexual fantasy – him Tarzan, you Jane – it should be swinging for both of you.

WHAT IF CHAMELEMAN IS YOUR PARTNER?

You have a challenge – but if you are married to him, you know that already. A bit of advice: as he gets older, Chameleman can forget who he really is. All those countless character and behaviour transformations can take their toll. Over the years, his core personality has multiplied so many times it's now buried from view, even from him. If that's the case, he will come to rely on you more and more, not least to remind him in which box he has ended up.

MOST LIKELY TO SAY

'Yes, I agree with you totally.'

KEY QUESTION

Chamelemen are usually to be found high up the social ladder. Do you join your one or do you watch from a distance, observing his nuanced movements?
Answer: Watch from a distance first, and then, if so inclined, join him, but with care.

CLUB MAN

Main characteristics

Clubbish; wears blazers, old school ties or football shirts; into brotherhoods and male bonding; happiest when he's with his club pals.

What's he like?

I once knew a man who prided himself on the fact that he'd never joined any club, 'not even the golf club', the implication being that he was just too independent of mind to want to join a club. Anyway, wasn't it one of the Marx Brothers who joked, 'I'd never join any club that would accept me as a member'? Much as I admire this sentiment, there is an attraction in being a member of some associations or clubs – most of us like to belong to something – but what do we make of the man who seems to exist only through the identity handed down to him by his club? This type of male is Club Man and there are quite a lot of them about.

Club Men are not that difficult to spot. For one thing, they have a tendency to advertise the fact that they have an association with something bigger and better than themselves. Their reasoning is that there is little point in being a member of an exclusive club unless those who aren't members have the opportunity to be just that teeny bit envious. So expect to see this type of guy wearing his club tie or blazer to work, sporting the latest Liverpool FC or Real Madrid shirt at weekends, or with a club sticker plastered to his car windscreen. He'll display anything that sends out a clear and unmistakable signal that he 'belongs'.

For Club Man to feel really good about himself, the higher profile the club the better. He's likely to prefer the colours of Manchester United to Rotherham United, and the scarf of Oxford University to Luton University. But this is just one aspect of the club that matters. Two other key factors are 'how exclusive is it?' and 'how expensive is it to get in?' Any club that has all three factors, such as the Garrick or St James's clubs in London, is right at the top of many Club Men's list. Oh, and there is an additional aspect that is equally if not more important – the club has to be male dominated, that is, run by men primarily for the benefit of men.

The psychology of it all is quite simple really. Clubs give Club Man something that we all need – an identity. He doesn't have to work too hard on his own identity, it is handed to him by his club. Club Man's sense of masculinity is enhanced through his association with something that is all male and yet grander and more élite than himself. The club link serves to elevate Club Man among the male fraternity, or at least, he believes that to be the case – the reality might be quite different. For some males, this sense of masculine superiority might be achieved through their university, say Oxford, Cambridge, Harvard or Yale; or it may be a Varsity club, the local golf club or a gentlemen's club in the city. Freemasons work especially well in this regard, being male dominated and long established, with applications by discreet invite only. In the UK, being a member of the House of Lords would do fine, or a member of the Marylebone Cricket Club – these are at the top of the English Club ladder. In the US, it would probably have to be the CIA, the Senate or the House of Representatives.

However, not all clubs are so obviously middle class and respectable as those mentioned. Lots of Club Men get their male identity from being members of less 'legit', more dangerous types of clubs. A good example would be youth gangs, such as those we see increasingly in the US and central America, or criminal gangs such as the Mafia and the Yakuza. It could even be Hell's Angels – to be surrounded by all that oil, leather, sweat and testosterone is a real turn-on for some Club Men.

Can Club Man be trusted in love?

Yes, usually. Having established that Club Man has some downsides to his personality, what are his more positive characteristics? Well, perhaps his simple character is itself an attraction. Not every woman wants to have to act as a sort of surrogate mother to male types such as Sigmund and Wallflower. Also, Club Man is strong on loyalty. However, yes, you guessed it, such loyalty is mainly given to his club. Club Men are much more likely to get divorced from their wives than they are from their club. These guys do not leave their clubs easily. Once they have been accepted, they are impressively faithful, never shifting one iota in their allegiance. Don't expect such loyalty inevitably to transfer to the home, and, most importantly, the bedroom. It might, but if you want to know whether Club Man is going to follow through on that come-on from the barmaid, you have to know about his club. If it's respectable and conservative, with a lot of ageing, doddery members, you are probably okay. If he does roam, it won't be because his mates at the club encourage it. Examples are the Freemasons and the House of Lords. But if his clubmates appear rather shag-happy, be careful.

Is Club Man romantic?

Romance is not one of his strongest points but in the initial stages of your affair he will make a concerted effort to impress. Don't expect him to be particularly imaginative as a seducer, and remember that those Club Men who are into football have an irritating habit of arranging the weekends in Paris or Madrid to fit in with matches.

Is Club Man the marrying kind?

Yes, although as I've said, if Club Man's clubmates are into playing away, he may well be too. Marriage or a partnership gives Club Man a certain respectability while signalling to his mates that he's straight, which is very important in a male-dominated club environment – to be found 'cruising' would definitely be the end of his membership. A further point to note is that Club Man is in reality rather afraid of women, of their response to him, if negative, and of his own possible inadequacy, be it sexual or emotional. By getting married, Club Man can largely negate, or at least not have to deal with, such potentially disruptive feelings towards the opposite sex.

What sort of woman does Club Man go for?

Firstly, Club Man wants a partner who doesn't give him too much grief over the time he spends with his mates down at the club. Secondly, he loves to have a woman on his arm who complements his club image. She must fit in. Thirdly, this type of man needs someone who will listen to him go on about his club. As an example, watch Club Men at parties. They can be really interesting to study. Even if they aren't wearing their club tie or T-shirt, it won't be long before they're telling you they are members of such and such a club. This desire to talk about their club a lot is because many never quite get over the fact that a particular club or association actually accepted them in the first place. They are pathetically grateful to have been given the okay to join and, once in, it's something they feel a real compulsion to broadcast. Much as this may make them feel good, it's not necessarily a good chat-up line at social gatherings. Women can get very suspicious about a bloke who only wants to talk about how happy he is when he's with his mates or whose general knowledge and intellect seem to extend to an analysis of a particular football team's performance. This is one of the key characteristics of Club Man – his is a very simple sort of masculinity. He really is an uncomplicated bloke. There is none of the complex depth you get with Jeffrey, none of the intensely ambitious, loner mentality you get with Murdoch, and none of the sensitive reflection you get with Libman.

What is Club Man like as a father?

Nothing pleases this male face more than to be able to get his offspring, ideally male ones, into his club. The pleasure he will get from taking his son to see his football team play or from putting his child's name down for his Alma Mater, such as Eton or Harrow, will know no bounds. However, regarding most other parental duties, Club Man is like many male faces, good in parts.

Could you work for Club Man?

Yes, provided you can put up with his extended rambles about how important his club is. He is not particularly obsessive about work and career, and nor is he likely to be a tough taskmaster. He's not one of the more complicated male faces, so once you've got his measure you should be able to handle him without too much difficulty.

Would you like Club Man as a friend?

Yes again, if you are in his club. However, social class plays a significant part in Club Man's sense of identity, so whether you are lower or higher up the social ladder can be important to this male face. Of course, not all Club Men aspire to being invited to join one of London's, Washington's or Paris's more exclusive gentlemen's clubs. Many settle for something a little more downmarket, which is where football comes in. With football clubs, it's just a matter of deciding which one to follow – no secret meetings are involved where your application is scrutinised by senior members late one night over cigars and brandy.

It's important to recognise that there are different levels of club membership, and friendship, at work, and they're inevitably linked to class or financial status. But whether Club Man is a brickie from Barnsley, or an alumnus of Harvard or Cambridge, the common factor that works for every Club Man is that it is through his association that he gets to feel like a proper man. If, through your friendship, you can help him achieve this otherwise elusive sense of maleness, he's one for you.

Scientifically speaking

Whichever club he has joined, it has to reinforce, and preferably raise up, Club Man's social status and position. Club Man's behaviour can be seen as an attempt to establish his identity through male bonding. The club has, as Jacques Lacan might say, a phallic dimension in so much as it is invested with male power and apparent potency. Men's masculinity is generally pretty fragile and therefore anything that gives it a bit of a boost is really quite important. Of course, this type of male psychology doesn't work just for Club Men; it works for other types of men as well. Indeed, many of the male faces described in this book will be members of some sort of club or, more likely, avid supporters of a football team or similar. When they visit the club, or go to the match on a Saturday afternoon, they are signalling their association with other men and the fact that they belong in this place called the 'man's world'.

Is Club Man the man for you?

It's easy to be a little unkind to Club Men, not least because they are so stereotypically male and rather shallow – all those heavily leathered bikers exhibiting outlandish masculinity like Mad Max on steroids. But it's also true that most Club Men are basically insecure and vulnerable – why else would they need approval from other men? So, should you be considering dating such a guy, or even marrying him? That needy side can be quite a turn-on for some women, to think that beneath all that clubbish, male posturing, here is a guy who really needs a woman's tender love and affection. Just be aware that marriage will only be on the cards if he thinks you'll be acceptable to his clubmates. Feminists need not apply.

To sum up

To understand Club Man you have to understand that his club is, in fact, a brotherhood. Consequently, for him, clubs are much more than somewhere to go two or three nights a week. They act to reinforce his male characteristics by signalling what he should wear, how he should behave, and even the sort of language to use. Think of some of the coded language used by the Mafia in the TV series *The Sopranos*. Clubs are a sort of comfort blanket for these guys, a place where they can retreat to the relative safety and certainty of clearly set out male rituals and behaviours. While this sort of male bonding works for many of the faces, Club Man is different because he takes it to extremes. If you observed him for any length of time, you'd probably come to the conclusion that he has little else in his life other than his club and his clubmates. If you can handle his particular obsession, and he considers you able to fit in, it could be a perfect partnership.

HOW TO SPOT A CLUB MAN

If he's not wearing his membership symbol around his neck or on his back, ask him what he does in his leisure time. Then just stand there and listen for the next half hour or so.

HOW DOES CLUB MAN PERFORM IN THE BEDROOM?

Thinks he's better than he actually is. Will likely need some coaching.

WHAT IF CLUB MAN IS YOUR PARTNER?

If you haven't already done so, it's probably not a bad idea to join your own club. Whether it's full of men or full of women is entirely your preference, depending on how you want to fill your own leisure time.

MOST LIKELY TO SAY

'Thursday nights I stay over at my club in the city.'

KEY QUESTION

When are they going to abolish the House of Lords?
Answer: Over his dead body (which may well turn out to be the case).

COOL POSER

Main characteristics

Sees himself as a very cool guy; into street cred; a good dancer; very fashion conscious; probably desires respect more than he desires sex.

What's he like?

Most men go through phases of being concerned about their appearance, depending on how well they are doing in the 'pulling' stakes. If they are riding the sexual and romantic roller-coaster, in general, men tend to give a little more consideration to how they think they look to the object of their desire. They might spend that bit longer choosing their next suit or jeans, and some may – and I stress may – even change their hairdresser. If, on the other hand, they have been married for aeons, many of the faces described here will not care too much if their hairstyle is a throwback to the Teddy Boy era of the 1950s and 1960s, or if their paunch looks as if it should be under observation in a maternity ward. Don't imagine that this principal works just for older men. Unfortunately it doesn't. I have seen many youths, supposedly in their physical and sexual prime, who look like their only hope of redemption is to give their complete wardrobe, and probably their bodies, to Oxfam.

However, there are some men for whom style is all – it is what defines them as males. No expense is spared in their extensive preparations for walking the streets in the expectation of admiring glances. No boutique is left unexplored in the search for that ever elusive iconic fashion item. These men are Cool Posers and they have one motto – 'Let no mirror be passed without a glance.'

Cool Poser is the style king of men, the peacock. Flamboyant and loud, this face works hard at being at the cutting edge of fashion. For him, his appearance signals his status and position in the world. His trousers will be baggier, wider, tighter, than any other bloke's. Every strand of his hair, even if covered by a fedora or a woolly hat, will be lovingly caressed into a display almost worthy of his hairdressing expenses. His trainers, ultimate symbols of his street cred, will be selected only after hours of careful consideration of what is 'in' or, more likely, what he expects to be next 'in'. It doesn't matter what the actual style is like, just so long as it is different – and 'cool'.

Some Cool Posers are so individualistic they would recoil in horror at the thought of being seen as part of a wider posse of 'cool' men. These Cool Posers exist in one place only – glossy magazines. Confident enough and with sufficient cash to dress in outlandish designer clothes, these trendsetters are often in showbusiness or international sport – premiership footballers are a prime example. Their media profile means they can get away with posing half-nude in chic French magazines, wearing a sarong, or changing their expensive hairstyles every few months, simply because they have an adoring public, and press, that follows their every fashion move. In the ranks of Cool Posers these men are at the top, they are the leaders rather than followers of fashion – they are the ones who set the style for the anonymous mass of Cool Posers to emulate. For most Cool Posers, any aspirations they may have to one day front *Hello* or *Cosmopolitan* magazines must remain, sadly for them, aspirations. But despite this lack of an international audience, the average Cool Poser does have his own means of acquiring a reputation as a fashion icon, even if it's only in his local neighbourhood.

Cool Poser is one of those male faces you can now see anywhere in the world. For example, if you find yourself in Hong Kong, Thailand or Singapore, you'll see young men who have decided to dye their hair an interesting shade of orange, presumably in the hope that it makes them look less, well, Chinese, Thai or Singaporean. In other words, they set out to look different – and they do, there is no doubt about it. Go to the cities of the US and Central America and you won't be able to miss the countless young Cool Posers, each one of whom is attired in local variations on a dress code of baggy clothes, reversed baseball caps, chains and tattoos. Apart from gesturing with their hands a lot when they talk, their language will be peppered with Latino, black or white rap and hip-hop slang – think Eminem or 2 Live Crew – thereby rendering it unintelligible to the average, usually older, citizen, which is largely its purpose.

But much as he might think so, Cool Poser is not a recent addition to male faces. He's been around for at least a few decades. In the UK, they used to be known as 'Boy Racers', and could be found speeding up the motorways or around city centres in souped-up hatchbacks, their GTIs laden with surprisingly powerful bass speakers. Like today's Cool Poser, this earlier version considered public transport very non-cool, underground trains excepted. So don't go looking for Cool Poser on buses or trains. His preferred mode of transport, if he can afford it, is likely to be a black BMW, which many refer to as 'Black Man's Wheels', or perhaps a silver Lexus for those who desire a less ubiquitous motor. This is one face who does not ride a bicycle, unless he's a wannabe Cool Poser of around 16 years old, in which case he may be found tripping along pavements on a BMW mountain bike.

Can Cool Poser be trusted in love?

Trust is not one of his strong points. He can be the sort of guy who really flatters you and gives you a strong sense of being special. He'll want to show you off to his mates and he can have quite an acute sense of how women, especially young women, think. But all this is part of his posturing. Most young Cool Posers are not looking for long-term commitment; they prefer short-term fun and good times. In the end, most women are let down by a Cool Poser, coming to grief on his ego and self-regard. Don't date this guy expecting it to be the big one; date him for fun. One further warning – if he starts getting emotionally abusive with you, don't put up with it. That sort of one-sided relationship can become a habit that many women slip into without realising it. Once Cool Poser thinks you'll always be there for him, no matter how badly he treats you, you've really got problems. Walk before you get to that point.

Is Cool Poser romantic?

As far as romance is concerned, it's a mixed offering with this face. Date him and you get to go to the coolest parties, the most fashionable clubs. Your holidays together will be taken at the hippest beach resorts. Wherever he goes, he carries an air of style as if the world is his oyster. If you are a woman who likes to be cool, Cool Poser would probably suit you well. Many times have I seen red-haired young Hong Kong Chinese couples walking hand in hand around expensive fashion stores, and looking so happy together, the perfect duos. Also, much as he likes to be with his mates, Cool Poser definitely wants to be seen as sexually attractive, though to which sex depends, of course, on his preferences. There are an extraordinary number of gay Cool Posers out there. So as a short-term partner, Cool Poser can work out quite well for many women. If you like your man to be smartly turned out and overtly macho, he's for you. He's going to have that swagger and roll intended to suggest a potent combination of confidence and testosterone and thus something of a stud in bed. However, as with all men, just how good he is between the sheets depends on his experience. As a guide, you can expect him to come up with the goods as required. Another warning – if he fails on this score do not, under any circumstances, tell him or, worse, his mates!

Is Cool Poser the marrying kind?

Cool Posers tend to be younger men, in their teens and twenties, and are not likely to be for settling down. They generally take a long time to mature – most likely into their forties – so avoid pushing this guy into saying 'I do', at least until his monthly spending on fashion and hairdressing has gone down to such a level as could sustain a mortgage and children. By this time, Cool Poser should have grown out of the need to dye his hair, adorn himself with pins and chains, or refer to his mates as 'homies'.

What sort of woman does Cool Poser go for?

Although Cool Poser is very switched on to how he looks, he is much less aware of his emotional depths, so he prefers younger women, those he can manipulate a little and who look up to him. He doesn't like women who are more intelligent than he is and who will question him about his behaviour. He can be quick to anger if he feels his manhood is threatened or if he is looked down upon by either sex, especially women. Also, that notorious green-eyed monster, jealousy, can easily take root. Cool Poser may well be able to 'talk the talk' with his mates, but don't expect him to be so open with you. Most Cool Posers do not have the drive, persistence and ambition of Alpha Male, although many would definitely like to see themselves in that mode, climbing the social ladder. He is, however, similar to Neanderthal in that if you are 'his woman', he will act in a pretty traditional male way. In his mind, you are his 'property' and he will want to protect you. He will expect to make most of the decisions – you can rely on him knowing which nightclubs to frequent, but not which bus to get home – and he will always pay for the night out. And he always, always does the driving. In short, his is a pretty uncomplicated sort of masculinity, and one that has been around, in one form or another, for a long time.

What is Cool Poser like as a father?

Fatherhood is not for him. He has too much clubbing to do before he's ready to settle down and assume parental responsibility for someone less mature than himself. Yet despite this, a lot of Cool Posers end up being fathers, at least biological fathers. They may rarely see their offspring and are even less likely to help pay for their children's many needs, but Cool Posers can get quite a thrill from siring children. The reason is that getting a woman pregnant suggests, to them, their sexual potency. This is sad because children are a lifelong love and commitment, not a fashion or gender statement. Alas, a lot of Cool Posers don't see beyond their quest for a cool self-image.

Could you work for Cool Poser?

Older Cool Posers can be good fun to work for, so long as they are working in an environment that suits their lifestyle. Examples are nightclubs, bars, hairdresser's, record shops, discos, with pop groups. Take them out of such work settings and often they don't appear so cool after all.

Would you like Cool Poser for a friend?

Friendship is very important in this man's life, but male friends, not female ones. Like Club Man, Neanderthal and Uniform Man, Cool Poser really needs to be around males – male bonding is key to his identity. Unless he's gay, Cool Poser would fervently deny he prefers men to women, but just watch him in his social setting. It is men he gravitates towards. Women are largely in the background or adornments to his fragile masculinity. If you are a bit of a Cool Poser yourself, you should get on fine. If, however, you find all that male display too shallow and tedious, walk on by.

Scientifically speaking

The concept of the 'cool pose' originates from research undertaken by American sociologist Richard Majors. He noted that some young men adopt demeanours, gestures, styles, languages, attitudes, practices and postures that, among their peers, improve or strengthen their self-esteem. For Cool Poser, the fact that these often macho displays may be rejected by wider society only serves to reinforce their importance. By being, as he sees it, at the cutting edge of fashion, Cool Poser earns respect within his own narrow, but influential, community of fellow men.

Is Cool Poser the man for you?

Despite all his efforts to appear a twenty-first century beau, many a Cool Poser finds he doesn't have that much success with women. His relationships, perhaps not surprisingly, tend to be brief, and his constant obsession with his appearance warns women of his vanity. Perhaps he cares too much about himself, and women sense this. Straight Cool Posers are at risk of appearing to be closet gays.

Maybe every woman should date a Cool Poser at some time in her life, preferably when she is young and up for the fun of it all; or date one when he has reached a more interesting and mature age and is about to become Alpha Male or Achilles. Otherwise watch out. This face has a habit of not taking women too seriously. In fact, treating women badly is, for many Cool Posers, a measure of their manhood. Be confident that with Cool Poser you'll get into the liveliest parties on the street and the coolest clubs, but do not assume you'll be going home with him at the end of the night.

If you fancy long-term commitment with a Cool Poser, the golden rule is to assess whether he is still wrapped up in all that posing, or whether he's ready to transform into a more mature male type. If it's the former, put him back on the shelf for a few years. If it's the latter, he could well turn out to be any of the more mature male faces on offer, eventually.

To sum up

Self-regarding and obsessed with display, young Cool Posers like to think of themselves as streetwise guys on the way up. It's no surprise that so many have youth gang connections because these give them the necessary platform from which to flaunt and parade themselves. But below the icy posture, 'bopping' walk and 'attitude', most Cool Posers are very insecure, if not shallow – this is no budding Preacher-like intellectual, and his daily reading is unlikely to be the broadsheet press. He might be expert at portraying indifference to all around him, but this is just to conceal his vulnerable ego. His is a world where respect is sought if not expected, but not always given. His self-esteem may be high when he's with his mates, but in less familiar settings it can crumble. Admire his fashionable look and cool language if you like, but recognise they are shields to protect him from an often hostile world.

HOW TO SPOT A COOL POSER

It's not difficult – every town and city has them, probably driving something flash.

HOW DOES COOL POSER PERFORM IN THE BEDROOM?

He won't be wearing Y-fronts, that's for sure. Less confident in bed than his cool pose manner would suggest, especially the younger version. However, he can get to be a performer once his confidence, and experience, builds up.

WHAT IF COOL POSER IS YOUR PARTNER?

Unlikely if he's still in his twenties, unless he's just stopping by and taking a break from all that clubbing for a few weeks or months. Don't get pregnant.

MOST LIKELY TO SAY

'Walk the walk, talk the talk.'

KEY QUESTION

Cool Poser has just bought a new car, something flashy, in keeping with his self-image. To whom does he show it off first – you, his mother or his mates?
Answer: His mates – they are the ones he's posing for.

CORPORATE MAN

Main characteristics

Relishes security; a follower not a leader; believes in mission statements; high on air miles; to be trusted – will always return home.

What's he like?

In the mid-twentieth century, a new type of male face emerged in society, a face that has come to epitomise middle America, middle Japan, middle England – in fact, middle everywhere. From rather quiet beginnings, this male type has so proliferated that he is now one of the most numerous. He has colonised every corner of the world, every organisation and every neighbourhood. There are millions of them out there and their numbers grow daily. He is Corporate Man.

The rapid rise of Corporate Man into the masculinity mainframe was triggered by the development of large, multinational corporations some fifty or so years ago. These bureaucratic, ubiquitous organisations now straddle the globe, and they give Corporate Man his primary identity. Their names and products are familiar to us. Indeed, without them there'd be no cars, no media, no leisure industry, no washing-up liquid, no burgers, no oil. We'd be back in the eighteenth and nineteenth centuries, tilling the land. So let's be grateful that Corporate Man is with us because without him life would be much less pleasant. He, above any other male face, has given us the modern world.

The man at the heart of the corporate treadmill is your archetypal middle-of-the-road guy. He may well follow sport, but he's not as obsessed with it as many Club Men. He drives a decent company car or people carrier, but secretly yearns to get his hands on a Honda S2000 or TVR. He has four weeks' holiday a year and usually takes two of them by the beach with his wife and kids. He knows how much his pension is worth and can predict his monthly income down to the last dollar or euro. However, money is not what drives him – as he sees it, his salary is merely fair reward for all those hours spent at the office. Unless it's dress-down Friday, expect to see Corporate Man every weekday morning at around 8.00 trundling off to work wearing his dark suit, white shirt and slightly adventurous tie. He shops at M&S or Next and lives in a nice neighbourhood in a comfortable family house surrounded by a neatly trimmed hedge or low brick wall.

Can Corporate Man be trusted in love?

The younger version of Corporate Man may appear rather flighty at times, a bit arrogant maybe, but don't be fooled by his behaviour in wine bars and lap-dancing clubs. He'll settle down as the years go by. He'll get greyer along with his hair. The incessant routine and security of office life will dull whatever secret desires he has to opt out and become a Backpacker. His life is on a fairly clear track and so long as he learns to duck and dive a little, so it will continue.

You can be fairly confident that Corporate Man is strong on dependability, trust and reliability. He is not so hot on creative imagination and ruthless competitiveness. He may well be a middle or senior manager in a company, but he's basically a follower, not a leader. His progress up the career ladder is steady rather than spectacular – not for him the giddy heights attained by Alpha Male. He doesn't have the artfulness of Chameleman and he's certainly no Murdoch. At around fifty, he'll be stuck reasonably high up the corporate ladder but going no further, precisely the point at which some Corporate Men start transforming into Manchild.

What most Corporate Men relish is constancy and security – things staying the same. Unfortunately for Corporate Man, they rarely do. Today, organisational life is much less secure than it used to be, so Corporate Man is having to adapt. With companies now regularly downsizing, he's having to learn to be a little more flexible in his career aspirations. Gone are the days when Corporate Man could expect to find himself a secure niche in one company and quietly live out his time until retirement at sixty-five. Now he has to move around a little, play the corporate game, and watch his back. But then, this is what he is best at – giving loyalty, giving his time, giving his life. So if you get involved with this guy, know that loyalty in relationships is one of his real strengths.

Is Corporate Man romantic?

Corporate Man can be as predictable in the bedroom as he is in the office. One woman I spoke to, who has been married to a Corporate Man for over twenty-five years, observed that while she was confident he'd never been unfaithful, there were times when she wished he had been. Why? Because, as she put it, 'the experience would probably do him good. Maybe make him a little more imaginative in bed.' All those years of daily commuting, petty office politics and business development plans have dulled her Corporate Man.

No expert at the gender game, Corporate Man's attitude towards women tends to be both limited and traditional. He sees men and women as being necessarily different, perhaps even from different planets, but ultimately complementing each other. Even gay Corporate Men tend to get married – coming out can be quite a high-risk strategy in many organisations. Corporate Men rarely make the change to being house-husbands, but, given the push, quite a few do come to enjoy being self-employed in their later years, albeit on a much lower income. Although we are seeing more Corporate Women than ever before, they are still very much a minority, so Corporate Man can expect that most of the women he comes across will be secretaries, cleaners or from Personnel. He's their boss rather than the other way round. Consequently, Corporate Man is often a little clumsy with women, being much more used to sending them emails than romantic endearments. So if you are considering dating a Corporate Man – and every woman does at some point in her life – recognise his limitations on the romance front. He may well need some guidance from you. Be patient.

Is Corporate Man the marrying kind?

Unlike Risker, Corporate man is not burdened with the itch to put his comfortable lifestyle on the line, and he has none of the complexities that trouble faces such as Sigmund. He is the very antithesis of Backpacker, although every Corporate Man would sometimes secretly love to tell his boss where to put his/her job and head off into the sun. But he can't do that. His company is almost like a family to him. It gives him a corporate identity, and a clear set of rules and expectations, and it rewards him for his efforts and for his loyalty. It provides a place where he feels he belongs. It is for these exact same reasons that marriage is so important for Corporate Man – he is one of the archetypal male marrying types.

With the corporation providing him with both his material and emotional support, Corporate Man has the ideal platform from which to go out and make his mark – but safely and without danger. Okay, so he is pretty predictable, but then he's dedicated to his work, and generally good at it. All those five-year plans, appraisals, performance indicators – they really mean something to him. As he sees it, they provide him with the tools with which to measure himself, and others. They are necessary. They tell him what he should be doing, and, mostly, how to do it. Corporate Man doesn't want to build an empire; his employers already provide him with one. All he has to do is dedicate his life to keeping their empire ticking over, functioning and profitable. And he does. As his wife, you will play a key role in keeping your Corporate Man safely on this straight, but predictable, path.

What sort of woman does Corporate Man go for?

Working in a large-scale organisation, Corporate Man is surrounded by fellow Corporate Men. This is one of the benefits to his masculinity. All these men together, day by day, week by week, year by year, serve to reinforce each other's male identity. They wear identical clothes, drive identical cars, speak an identical language – corporate jargon. In fact, if you look carefully, you'll see that they even marry identical wives – women who are safe, reliable, dependent and who make excellent mothers; women who put their husbands and families first. This is Corporate Man's ideal soulmate.

What is Corporate Man like as a father?

In the UK, fathers of under-fives are now spending on average two hours a day with their children, compared to the fifteen minutes their fathers and grandfathers did. This is good news for everyone, especially the kids. The male face most likely to be doing this increased parenting role, along with Libman and Teddy Bear, is Corporate Man. Research shows that many Corporate Men would spend even more time at home if only their bosses, mostly Alpha Males, would permit it. We can speculate that if all the male faces were as potentially good at being fathers as Corporate Man, perhaps there would be fewer social problems among male youth.

Corporate Man may not be the most imaginative of male faces, but when it comes to family life, his desire for security and stability really helps. He is a man who is into routine and predictability and while these traits may annoy some people, they are just what his kids need, especially in their teenage years. Sure, Corporate Man may occasionally be too stressed to make the time for bedtime reading to his kids, but this is one male face you can generally rely on to undertake his share of the parenting role.

Could you work for Corporate Man?

The likelihood is you already do. Just look around at the male middle and senior managers in your organisation. Undoubtedly, several Corporate Men are in that bunch somewhere. Some of these men may not appeal to you, but remember, without them the organisation would not function so effectively. It's also worth reflecting on Corporate Man's difficult position, situated as he is between hard-driving Alpha Males at the top and the rest of us at the bottom. Corporate Man wants to keep us all happy, if only for a quiet life. However, this attempt to be all things to all people rarely pays off, which tends to result in him feeling a little squashed, if not a little undervalued. Caught in the middle is not always the best place to be, so be patient when he has his off days.

Would you like Corporate Man as a friend?

Go to your local golf club on a Sunday morning and you will see numerous Corporate Men doing their thing with their mates. For these precious few hours they are blissfully happy – no memos, no emails, no meetings, just a little white ball and a lot of holes. Back in the bar after the 18th, Corporate Man is quite a social animal. He likes to be around people, which is why so few of them really enjoy early retirement – just what can they do with all that time on their hands?

Scientifically speaking

As British sociologists Deborah Kerfoot and Jeff Hearn have argued, throughout the world, organisational and managerial roles have traditionally been dominated by males and as a consequence are very masculine in their culture and practice. Despite increasing numbers of women in management, this continues to be the case. It is within this gendered world that Corporate Man achieves his primary sense of masculine identity. For him, it is largely a seamless process – being a man and being a manager. When Corporate Man walks into his office, he is getting some confirmation of himself as a male, and a relatively powerful one at that.

Is Corporate Man the man for you?

Does this type of man attract you or would you run a mile from such middle-class normality? Well, on the plus side, although

Corporate Man may be prone to cracking sexist jokes in the office, and while he may like his dose of vanilla porn on a Friday night, he won't roam far. He's no philanderer. His company may send him across the world on business trips, and you could well find him and his Corporate Mates chancing a visit to the Bangkok girly bars of Pat Pong or the sex district of Amsterdam, but beneath the loud male bravado they'll be nervous. It's not really their style.

Within the organisation, Corporate Man generally gets on better with men than with women. His male underlings tend to appreciate his uncomplicated masculinity while his Alpha Male bosses know he's dependable and not power-hungry, so he's no threat to them. However, women employees, especially clever, ambitious ones, can get very frustrated with his desire to play by the rules and his inherent sexist attitude – ditto this in spades if his boss is a woman. Indeed, underneath the apparently worldly exterior is a man who can crumble when strong-minded women question his decisions at work, although he's quite okay with his wife being in charge of the house. He would argue that his world is increasingly a fast paced one, demanding, stressful and challenging, and that men are better suited to run it than women. He is wrong, of course. But despite such attitudes, and the pressures of work, he is likely to be a loyal and loving family man, not least because he knows that without his wife behind him, providing the domestic setting on which so much of his endeavours rely, he'd be up the creek. As his wife or partner, this is the world you have opted into.

To sum up

Corporate Man is most comfortable in his own bed, snuggled up to the familiar contours of his wife, the children soundly asleep in their respective bedrooms. Marry him for the predictability of it all and for the final salary pension scheme, not for excitement and passion.

HOW TO SPOT A CORPORATE MAN

Aspiring Corporate Men, in their last year at university, can be found visiting undergraduate career fairs, heading for the exhibition stands of large corporate employers. Older Corporate Men can be found washing their cars, tending their gardens or on the golf course at weekends. They tend to be quite good at DIY.

HOW DOES CORPORATE MAN
PERFORM IN THE BEDROOM?

Dependable, steady, reliable, but don't expect an early night more than once a week.

WHAT IF CORPORATE MAN IS YOUR PARTNER?

Have his children and buy yourself a 4x4 in which to cart them around. If you ever decide to inject a little extra-marital excitement into your life, your Corporate Man will never guess. He's just too busy at the office.

MOST LIKELY TO SAY

'Can I have an upgrade?'

KEY QUESTION

When it comes to buying clothes, does he spend hours browsing the designer boutiques, or is it a quick visit to M&S?
Answer: He hates shopping, much preferring you to buy his clothes for him.

GADGETMAN

Main characteristics

A real techno-freak; good with all his fingers; poor eyesight; insular and socially inept; contented in a sad sort of way.

What's he like?

One aspect of the twenty-first century that no one can get away from is technology. Whether you plough a paddy field in Bali or shepherd llamas in the Andes, you will never be far from the Internet. Knowing this may drive you slightly mad or give you a warm feeling of comfort. I guess that all depends on how you feel about computers. Most of us have a so-so relationship with them, but I do know people who cannot abide them. One such person is a close friend of mine, an internationally renowned academic who has written several books, but who still can't use email. Whenever he's faced with anything remotely high, or even low, tech, his sharp mind goes into spasms. For him, the pen is indeed mightier than the laptop. While most of us would have some sympathy with my friend's plight, not least because we've experienced similar emotions ourselves when trying to open a particularly intransigent Word attachment, there is one man out there for whom technology is everything. Without it, he wouldn't exist. Sure, he has a physical presence, a body like everyone else, but his character, his inner personality, has long since succumbed to the addictive temptations that lurk in the netherworld of e-space. He is Gadgetman.

Sometimes known as geek or nerd, modern day Gadgetman, especially the younger version, spends endless hours transfixed in front of his computer screen, playing the latest video games, fathoming the intricacies of Firewire, watching the world from a distance. He is fascinated by the latest electronic gadgetry, which he deftly operates and avidly collects. For Gadgetman, the Internet has proved to be his saviour, for through it he can collect a sense of identity, membership of the global community – and some social respectability – without ever leaving his bedroom. A few Gadgetmen have managed to combine their obsession with gadgets and technology with an ability to make money – they were astute, or lucky, enough to catch the moment and ride the new technology tiger – which is how we've come to have Microsoft, Opera and Google making our trips into e-space so much easier.

Although it may seem strange and inexplicable to some – my academic friend included – Gadgetman's world is in essence fairly simple. With technology, everything is in a box the contents of which can be taken out, assessed, measured and put back in again – quite scientific really. So long as you have the patience and desire, and some basic knowledge, this technology can be understood by anyone. Most of us may not see the point of knowing what goes on in a SIM card or understanding precisely how 7,500 songs can be stored and played on something the size of a large matchbox and called an iPod, but for Gadgetman these are serious imponderables that need to be solved.

Can Gadgetman be trusted in love?

Much as we might admire Gadgetman's GameBoy skills or keyboard dexterity, most of us remain slightly suspicious of a man who lives a large part of his life in a James Bond or Tomb Raider fantasy world, a place where Lara Croft is much more real and sensual than Kylie Minogue ever could be. This sort of masculine obsessiveness suggests a rather shady, undeveloped personality. To be sure, Gadgetman may be emotionally and socially immature, but in terms of trusting him not to go off with your best friend he's not a problem. He gets his real kicks from pursuing digital fantasy female characters rather than the more complex real thing.

Is Gadgetman romantic?

He may be a dab hand at building an all-destroying mini-robot, and he'd no doubt be quite articulate at telling you how it works, but don't ask him to explain why some men prefer to spend their time with machines rather than with their wives. Moreover, don't ask him which he loves most – the machine or his lover. This lack of self-awareness is one of Gadgetman's real weaknesses – he has a very underdeveloped emotional intelligence.

In this respect, Gadgetman is typical of several male faces. He relates best to objects he can scrutinise carefully, inspect, adjust, tamper with, modify, improve, take apart, things that are manageable but need a screwdriver taken to them every so often. That's why he's not too good with women and usually pretty hopeless at romance. Having the skill to destroy Wario's monster enemies may delight him but such useful talents are, alas, of little help when it comes to forming and sustaining relationships. Gadgetman knows how machines work, why they do what they do, how they can be made to do something different. He's much less confident about the female mind – an entity that is, for him, definitely from another planet.

Is Gadgetman the marrying kind?

Mostly, Gadgetman tends to remain single and with his mum until some doughty, resolute female sets eyes on him and decides he's worth the risk. Maybe she's into fantasy worlds just like he is. The older Gadgetman is likely to be married with a family, attempting to balance competing demands on his time, such as work, wife, kids and the latest computer games. For these Gadgetmen, the age of the Internet really did make a difference to their married lives. With the onset and general acceptance of the technology, no longer did Gadgetman have to suffer the derision of his neighbours when attaching a 30ft radio mast to his garage so as to improve his long-wave radio frequency connections. Similarly, his days and nights of being exiled to the garden shed by his wife were at an end. He was invited back in the house, blinking, appreciative, a little bewildered, but now with a computer comfortingly installed in the spare bedroom. Modern-day Gadgetman, once Radio Ham, was relishing no longer being dismissed as an obsessive embarrassment by his family, most of whom didn't share his passion for listening to obscure radio messages passed back and forth across the globe by lonely, bearded men. No, sometime in the 1990s Gadgetman came in from the cold, suddenly welcomed by his wife as the one man who could help her reconfigure her crashed computer and explain MSN – and all for free.

What sort of woman does Gadgetman go for?

A woman who is just like him would be ideal. Unfortunately, or fortunately, there are fewer Gadgetwomen around than Gadgetmen, so he has to settle for someone altogether more socially rounded and mature. Such partnerships are very healthy for Gadgetman, although he doesn't always appreciate being dragged away from his PC to spend the weekend with his future in-laws.

In terms of the more intimate aspects of your relationship, if you do find yourself wrapped up with Gadgetman, you should not be surprised if he turns out to be more into fantasy sex than the sweaty, messy real thing. Don't blame him too much for this. Sex cannot be avoided on the Internet. Indeed, it drives the whole thing. Given this, it is to be expected that Gadgetman will be fairly experienced at navigating his way around some quite bizarre and interesting sites. Alas for Gadgetman, sex is one area where solo 'hands-on' practice does not necessarily translate into real-time finesse. So just how accomplished he'll be once he's in close proximity to your own interesting sites remains open to question.

What is Gadgetman like as a father?

He spends a lot of his time at home, so, at least theoretically, he is available to lend a hand with childcare duties. However, weaning him away from his PC long enough to take the kids swimming on a Saturday morning could still prove something of a challenge. It's not that Gadgetmen are bad fathers; it's just that they have such a narrow vision of life their children can be neglected. On the plus side, Gadgetmen will be only too happy to spend hours showing their kids how to use a computer. You'll need quite a large spare room for them all to fit in of an evening.

Could you work for Gadgetman?

The question is unlikely to arise. Gadgetmen are not inclined to be bosses, unless they inadvertently find themselves promoted to managing the IT department, in which case, they should be very supportive , not too authoritarian and quite uninterested in what goes on beyond their banks of computers.

Would you like Gadgetman for a friend?

Despite his weird lifestyle and insular behaviour, Gadgetman has a few good points and friendship is one of them. He makes a good friend. He'll always remember your birthday – reminded by e-cards; he'll be only too happy to install your virus protection and sort out your server – it makes him feel so masculine to fix things; and you'll never have to pop down to the travel agents again to book your holiday.

Scientifically speaking

It can be argued that Gadgetman suffers from a condition known as Asperger's Syndrome – a mild form of social autism. This may sound extreme but in fact it is very common, especially among young males. In Japan it has almost reached epidemic levels. In that country, which for some time now has been the best place to observe the impact of technology, several million teenaged Gadgetmen have opted out of the real world altogether, choosing instead to retreat to the insular comfort and security of their bedrooms, often for years on end. As their parents fear for their sanity, their children, and it's nearly always boys, are leading hermit-like lives, repelling intruders, their only access to the wider world being their computer screens. They are called *hikikomori,* which is Japanese for those who display 'acute social withdrawal' symptoms.

Is Gadgetman the man for you?

If, like Gadgetman, you've decided you prefer the virtual world to the real one, he'd probably make the ideal lover or partner.

Think of all those cosy nights, curled up in front of the PC screen, opening new windows together. You are likely to find him at the games counter of your local Virgin or HMV store. Pop along there and make like you're checking out the latest Playstation 2 games. If that doesn't work, try to get his email address and make contact with him through that. Tell him you want some help with your Firewall. You are sure to get a response. If you can prise him away from his laptop long enough to develop a real-time relationship, you'll likely have a steady and reliable man in your life – he's too engrossed in his gadgets to be bothered roaming, and with his computer skills he'll never be out of work. Just make sure you're connected to the Internet in the marital bedroom.

To sum up

Through his computer, Gadgetman inhabits a bizarre but extremely macho world where men are always strong, always fast, always virile, and always attractive to women. Yet while many male faces, and a few female ones, may well get a thrill from their weekly excursion into the manic, violent world of, say, a Grand Theft Auto Vice City game, only Gadgetman has divorced himself from the real world and taken up permanent residence in this virtual one. The twenty-first century is, indeed, his time.

HOW TO SPOT A GADGETMAN

Look for a man who always carries one of those pocket-computer thingies with him wherever he goes and who just loves to tell you how it works.

HOW DOES GADGETMAN PERFORM IN THE BEDROOM?

Well, it's possible he's learnt some interesting stuff from all those hours spent on the Internet, but that just shows he's better with the theory than the practice. So I'm afraid you'll have to take the lead between the sheets.

WHAT IF GADGETMAN IS YOUR PARTNER?

So how exactly did you manage to prise him away from his bedsit and computer long enough to get into a relationship? Well done. Hope you are enjoying your on-line games together.

MOST LIKELY TO SAY

'Damn, it's crashed again.'

KEY QUESTION

Can you live with a man whose idea of a good night out is a good night in with Google?
Answer: Yes you can, just so long as you can handle the predictability of it all.

JEFFREY

Main characteristics

Enjoys a world of make-believe; lives with half-truths, neither fact nor fiction; a social animal in search of acceptance; bewildering but compelling character.

What's he like?

Every male face has a unique character, its own little idiosyncrasies, and something that both attracts and detracts. That is the beauty of love. We fall for what we sense as different, as special; we fall for both the good and the not-so-good in a person – that unique combination of factors that makes the individual. However, there is one man who attracts women and men to him like no other, someone whom everyone is happy to know and befriend. Of all the faces, this is one of the easiest to love. In the grown-up world of men, this face is forever the little boy, the Peter Pan, never quite making it to adult masculinity, always getting into scrapes, yet always full of *joie de vivre*. He is Jeffrey.

If you stand back and look at the twenty-seven faces of men, you can see that they all have a part, a role to play. Taken together, the faces form a composite, a whole. Most aspects of the human condition are reflected in these faces. Whether this is by accident or design is impossible to say, but it does have a certain symmetry, and this is where Jeffrey fits in. He is our other half – the mischievous, cheeky, gifted, slightly devious, unaccountably reckless fellow we would all like to be now and again but for the most part can't because we are too conservative, insecure and hesitant. We play safe, so we need a face who can live our adventures for us, whose escapades we can follow, someone we can laud and admire, but on whom we can sit in judgement when they go too far. This is Jeffrey's role in life – to be our alter ego.

To understand Jeffrey, first you have to recognise that he is not just one person, he is countless people. He is a bit like Chameleman in that he has the ability to live his life in sealed boxes, compartments, slipping effortlessly from one to the other. The difference is that Chameleman knows he has this gift and tends to use it intentionally. By contrast, Jeffrey is very innocent, and this is what makes him so attractive. Here is a man who can be so many things to so many different people, and yet remain open-faced to the world and complete in himself. What a talent! Jeffrey is, I suppose, the twenty-first century equivalent of Walter Mitty: a multifaceted character whom few people truly understand, a man who lives in his very own private make-believe world, but who appears to be so rooted in ours. Jeffrey can live and thrive in the real world, often being the centre of attention, a career builder, devoted husband, caring father, party-giver, president of his golf club, and yet he also lives in a bubble, a private space that no one ever enters, a place even he does not fully recognise exists.

Don't imagine that Jeffrey has engineered it this way. He hasn't, it's just happened. He hasn't set out to be a multifaced person – that would be much too Machiavellian for him – so don't spend too much time trying to fathom out just how and why Jeffrey has constructed this impenetrable vacuum around himself. Just accept that there are some things about these faces we can never fully know, and that's certainly true of Jeffrey. Sure, it's reasonable to assume that Jeffrey's many faces are a form of protection, but from what? Here we can only speculate. Perhaps it all stems from a deep fear of rejection. Maybe he came from a desperately poor background as a child, or was rejected by his parents. Perhaps he was an abandoned baby, an orphan, an outcast at school. Whatever his early, character-forming experiences, they've certainly had a very profound effect on him as an adult. Rather than subject himself to such feelings of inadequacy and rejection again, Jeffrey has learned to become an over-achiever, a man on a mission of self-aggrandisement. He can never have too much money, never have too many friends, never have too many high-level social contacts. He must live the adventure, at whatever cost.

Can Jeffrey be trusted in love?

Given Jeffrey's complex character, it should come as no surprise that love is very central to his life. In fact, Jeffrey does love big-time. What's more, unlike many male faces, Jeffrey would be the first to admit his need for, and reliance on, another's affections. In fact, he can be quite an emotionally literate male. Perhaps Jeffrey recognises that while he may have different faces, at his core he is just a lost boy in search of love. He has a very young, open heart. Jeffrey can, then, be a unique and special partner. If he falls in love with you, there can be no escape. You will have to be his. He will certainly be yours – always. However, that commitment does not, alas, always translate into being faithful. So no, you cannot wholly trust him. Be prepared for him getting into many scrapes, occasionally with other women. This is something you may find impossible to tolerate, but the best way to deal with it is just to accept him for what he is, for the many faces he is. Don't condemn him when he lets you down. It's not done maliciously, with intent to hurt. It's just that he's caught up in so many different lives he can't always be relied on like other faces can. Whatever happens in his life, good or bad, he will always come home to you. He is no Backpacker.

Is Jeffrey romantic?

There is a bit of the showman in Jeffrey so expect romance in a way you never thought possible in a man. Nothing is too good for the woman in his life. No expense will be spared in making her feel wonderful, valued above all others. If you get emotionally and physically caught up in his mad, exclusive world, just go with it. Don't try to resist. You are on a rollercoaster and so long as you hold on tight you will be safe. But don't, whatever you do, try to alter him. This is one man you cannot change. He will be Jeffrey all his life.

Is Jeffrey the marrying kind?

Most certainly. Singledom is not for him. He will be very careful about whom he chooses as a partner and you should be equally careful before you say 'I do'. Divorce is not on his agenda so you'll likely be stuck with him for the duration. You could do worse.

What sort of woman does Jeffrey go for?

Jeffrey is a very special male face and he needs a very special partner. He will look for someone who attracts admiring glances, complements his well-honed social skills, and appreciates a good party. His perfect partner will be someone from higher up the social ladder than himself, an elegant educated woman who attracts attention in a respectful, subtle way. Most importantly, she should be very patient and loving.

What is Jeffrey like as a father?

Being a father is one thing Jeffrey usually gets right, although how he does this job when so many other men struggle is rather strange and difficult to understand. It probably comes from his sense of being not quite mature or grown-up. He really is good at playing the little boy and children can appreciate this. He can very easily inspire love and loyalty in his kids, especially in those moments of crisis in Jeffrey's life when all looks bleak and desperate. At times like these, his family will gather round to protect him. They all know he is the real child of the family and will always remain so.

Could you work for Jeffrey?

As much as he makes a good father, he makes a less than good boss. He is not a competent organiser of people, he struggles to delegate and he lacks patience. Despite all this, he can motivate his staff and encourage feelings of loyalty in them. However, his habit of telling half-truths can make them feel cheated and let down. In terms of organisational politics, Jeffrey can be very skilled, although he has to be careful not to spin too many different yarns to too many different people. If he can manage to keep all his friends and colleagues on track and believing in him, Jeffrey can work wonders in any setting. If you work for him, just go with the dynamics of it all, but be prepared to jump ship should the reef suddenly loom up unexpectedly.

Would you like Jeffrey as a friend?

Jeffrey is one of the most accomplished male faces at making friends, and also one of the most adept at losing them. This is one of Jeffrey's tragedies – he wants to be loved and liked, yet so often finds himself struggling to be accepted.

The house in the country, the big car and holidays in Mauritius are pleasures Jeffrey will wallow in, but his real aim in life is not to surround himself with material comfort. What he really yearns for is admiration and respect. He wants to be just like us, but more so. This desire for normality becomes a trap from which Jeffrey cannot escape. He wants to be accepted as an ordinary guy, but it's something he is completely incapable of achieving. In fact, he actually hates the ordinary, mundane world that most of us inhabit. He is blessed, or cursed, with a restless, dynamic energy that forces him to skip from situation to situation, always pushing his limits, forever testing himself, never being satisfied with what he has. He can never stop. In his pursuit of being everybody's friend, in his insatiable desire for respect and admiration, Jeffrey has to try to be something to everyone and in the process he stops being himself. Jeffrey has the ability to mirror what he sees in the outside world, but he can never be fully part of it. He plays out roles he thinks we want to see, for that is the way he gets us to like him, to accept him, but in so doing he remains apart from us – always trapped on the outside looking in.

Scientifically speaking

The German philosopher Friedrich Nietzsche wrote, 'Every philosophy conceals another philosophy; every opinion is also a hiding place; every word a mask.' He could have been describing Jeffrey – a man who does not exist except in his own fevered imaginings, a man whose life is a pantomime. If Jeffrey has a core identity, it is virtually indiscernible to the outside world. To a large extent, it is indiscernible to him as well. Much of his life is an attempt to reconcile and manage this paradox of being everything and nothing.

Is Jeffrey the man for you?

You may not have a Jeffrey in your life or among your circle of friends, but you will know of one. The likelihood is you'll have seen his name crop up now and again in the press – someone achieving amazing things yet always seemingly in trouble. He lives a larger-than-life existence, outside the realms, and the rules, that surround the rest of us. In many ways, he lives out our fantasies for us, and we secretly love him for it.

On balance, there are more pluses for living life with Jeffrey than there are minuses, which is why women who are married to one tend to stick it out. For one thing, life around Jeffrey is never, ever boring. He brings a joyfulness to his life and his relationships that few other male faces can. An added bonus is that he can be quite a highly sexed man – the physical act of making love gives him a sense of unity and purpose that is otherwise very elusive in his life, which is largely the reason he likes repeating the experience at regular intervals. If you think you can hold him, why not give it a go? But strap yourself in securely.

To sum up

Here is a man who name drops without a blush, conceals much more than he reveals, and conjures fantasy from fact with the skill of an author of best-selling fiction. But his closest friends and loved ones eventually come to realise that every high-powered friend that Jeffrey has is not only a protection against the cold outside world, he or she is also a part-time player in his unique and carefully constructed fantasy world, best described as 'faction' – fact and fiction combined. So if you decide to enter his bizarre world of multiple mirrors and hidden spaces, remember that Jeffrey enlists people into his fantasies in order to make such fantasies appear more real to him. He uses people, but usually in the nicest, most generous way. His whole life is devoted to building this amazing world of compelling make-believe. Is this sad or attractive – or both? We despair at his half-truths, but relish his stories. We are affronted by his lack of shame, but admire his tenacity. We marvel at his adventures, but condemn him when he steps over the line. We sense his insecurity, but what the hell, who isn't insecure?

HOW TO SPOT A JEFFREY

Look in the tabloids.

HOW DOES JEFFREY PERFORM IN THE BEDROOM?

Fantasy time with this one. Will want lots of sex and will be prepared for all sorts of fun and games. A real swinger, given half the chance. If you can't keep up with him, he's likely to go elsewhere.

WHAT IF JEFFREY IS YOUR PARTNER?

No one will ever love you like he does. Just hold on tight.

MOST LIKELY TO SAY

'Not everyone knows this, but Diana and I were very close.'

KEY QUESTION

Does he intend to write a novel?
Answer: If he doesn't, he should do. Just make sure you get to spend the advance.

JESTER

Main characteristics

Loves laughter; an audience freak; prone to being melancholy; a party animal; every day is Christmas Day with this face.

What's he like?

The best relationships work when both parties are able to function as a team. No, I don't mean one person is boss and the other does the job, but that both parties operate in a cohesive and self-supportive manner. Now, given that life can be such a test at times, wouldn't it be nice to have a significant other who is always there with a laugh and a joke, someone with a smile on his face, light and joyful? Well, yes it would. After a while some may find it grating, always having to laugh at a constant stream of jokes, but for many people, living with someone who has a highly developed sense of humour is to live with the perfect partner. A few men have such humour and laughter down to a fine art. They are called, unsurprisingly, Jesters.

Jester is the comic of the male faces, always up for a laugh, always ready with a telling anecdote or joke, an indispensable asset at any party. Not only is Jester a superb humorist, he's the best reliever of tension you'll ever find, almost as good as a sensual massage. When the kids get too much to handle, the cat has gone missing, or your boss is acting up again, Jester will invariably find the funny side to these trying moments in your life. He can take the mundane and downright irritable and transform them into fun and light-heartedness. Jester is the perfect antidote to the stress and tension of modern life.

To what extent Jester himself is ever under stress is more difficult to determine. He's one of those male faces who hides his feelings really well. So be aware that his humour and jokes may conceal deeper emotions. Jester uses humour not only to make friends and lighten situations, he occasionally uses it to cover up his inner, unresolved tensions and anxieties. The more confused and uncertain he is, the more jokes he tells. So remember, although Jester may laugh a lot in public, when he's not in front of an appreciative audience he may be quite melancholy, only a joke away from a real downer. Some Jesters can be like the clown with tears in his eyes – apparently smiling but with sadness lingering around them. In a way, this reveals one of the core characteristics of this male face – he may be an antidote to life's more difficult situations, but he is often a deep character, a man who is concerned to ensure other people are happy before himself. His motto is, 'If my loved ones and friends are happy, then so am I.'

Can Jester be trusted in love?

If you are in a relationship with Jester, you'll likely be happy and content, despite the fact that other women like him. However, if you are of a jealous disposition, Jester is not for you. His popularity with women will probably come to unsettle and disturb your equilibrium. When he smiles at and laughs with other women you'll never be sure if he's doing it to please or to seduce. Most Jesters just like to be liked, although a few cannot say no to a pretty face. So if you are of an untrusting nature, don't put yourself through this agony. Look elsewhere.

Is Jester romantic?

With their open and approachable manner, Jesters can do quite well in the game of love and romance. Women value Jester's ability to make light of a potentially tense situation, and to bring humour into romance. He's the sort of bloke who will get you smiling and laughing in no time and, as many women will agree, nothing seduces quite so well as laughter. But don't imagine that Jester uses his humour as a means to an end. He doesn't approach life in such a calculating way. Humour for him is a constant, a way of relating to others. If as a consequence women are attracted to him, that's a bonus – unless he's already in a relationship, in which case it may not be.

Is Jester the marrying kind?

Jesters can be very lonely and insular if they've no love in their life, so this is one male face who relishes a permanent, loving relationship. Getting to that point can, however, be a little troublesome with this face. He's not the most emotionally switched on of the male types and you may well have to be patient with him as he grows out of his juvenile masculinity. He'll get there over time, but his desire to be liked and to inspire laughter in others, while a lovely trait, hardly lends itself to mature considered reflection. In short, he's just too busy trying to be the clown of the party to stop for a while and think about what's going on for him as a man.

What sort of woman does Jester go for?

Someone who appreciates his jokes and sense of humour – otherwise it's hardly likely to be a long-term romance. Remember that underneath all the joking, here is a man who is quite unsure of himself, at least emotionally, and who needs an audience to confirm that he is liked, nice and appreciated. If you can play this role in his life, and still provide him with the emotional grounding he so badly needs, he'll love you like no other.

What is Jester like as a father?

He can make a superb father of under twelves, but as his off-spring move into puberty and teenagerdom things can go awry with this male face. As young children, his kids will love his sense of humour and playfulness. However, as they get older they will find it very annoying still being the butt of his jokes. Moreover, his teenaged son or daughter will find it very non-cool to have a dad who is always trying to play the clown. Once his kids are grown-up, they may come to see that their dad is a much more complicated and interesting character than they'd thought.

Could you work for Jester?

The Jesters I have come across have mainly been in jobs that require contact with the public and some sensitivity when dealing with people, rather than bosses at the top of the corporate ladder. They do especially well as taxi drivers, pub landlords, customer relations personnel and sales reps. However, Jesters can be found in other working environments, especially where a lot of men work together, such as engineering, building and manufacturing. The male camaraderie of the shopfloor gives Jester a particularly comfortable platform from which to weave his special magic. Not surprisingly, some Jesters even take the plunge and become pro or semi-pro stand-up comics, working nightclubs and pubs for a living, perhaps even going much further up the showbusiness ladder.

Jester's constant desire to be liked and accepted means that he's unlikely to be a politician or policeman, or to be working in a professional field that requires prolonged serious thought and mental application. He will not be a university researcher, lawyer, accountant or judge. The gravitas required for such roles is beyond Jester. In fact, gravitas is something he doesn't do at all well, certainly not for more than, say, two minutes. Jester sees the world in fairly simple terms but don't think that he's a simpleton. He isn't. What he cannot abide is the dour, the sombre and the grim.

Would you like Jester as a friend?

His outgoing and gregarious character ensures that Jester has a wide circle of friends. People warm to his openness and lack of edge. He is easy to be around and unlikely to lose his temper unless under a lot of pressure. He is not a prickly or morose character in the way that, say, Sigmund can be, and he's the very opposite of Mr Angry. If Jester finds himself having to deal with difficult people he invariably eases the tension by making a quip, even if it's at his own expense. He's not a confrontational type of guy. He tends to look for the best in people and will stay loyal to his friends even if they let him down, which they may occasionally do.

Scientifically speaking

The British sociologist Ian Craib suggested that all adults experience contradictory feelings of intimacy and trust in their relationships. As a result of infant experiences, we have largely irresolvable anxieties over loss, abandonment, exposure, desire, fear, love and hate. All adults grapple with these tensions, which arise from the psychological inheritance of childhood. Jester lives out exactly these contesting emotional needs in a very public way. He seeks love and acceptance through the approving gaze of his audience, while at the same time he flirts with the psychological dilemmas that arise from rejection and disapproval.

Is Jester the man for you?

As his partner you have to let Jester perform. The social world is his natural habitat. This is no insular individual; he loves an audience. People and laughter are his oxygen, so any woman who tries to deny him these will not be for him. Jester is best with those women who are trusting, relaxed and very confident in their relationships. If you're in love with a Jester, it's probably because of his social popularity, his desire to please, but most of all, his ability to make you laugh. You will no doubt also be appreciative of the fact that here is a man who doesn't put himself first. However, there will definitely be times when you find his jokes just a little irritating, and most Jesters have difficulty in reading people's moods – they tend to think that a little humour works in every situation when it certainly doesn't. So these aspects of his character may not always please you. You may also come to find that your Jester's light-hearted approach to life doesn't help when you're struggling to balance the family budget, sort out the kids' schooling, or plan your next house move. So be aware that Jester is not the type to fret or lose a night's sleep over the big issues in life. He much prefers, indeed he needs, a partner who can balance his frivolous approach to life with some weightiness.

To sum up

Everything considered, I guess Jester is one of the easiest faces to love, one of the nicest to be around. He may not be a leader of men, or of anything for that matter, but it won't trouble him. He is a social animal, not a political one. He could only get so far up the career ladder before he fell off laughing! What he is is steady, reliable, friendly and full of humour. Okay, he's a little irresponsible at times, but he's rarely grim and depressing – at least in public. Remember that the tears of the clown can be especially troubling, and as his wife or partner you'll see them now and again, but the clouds will invariably pass and once again all will be well in Jester's world.

HOW TO SPOT A JESTER

Don't look for him, just listen out for him. He's never far away. Won't be carrying the *Guardian* or the *New York Times*.

HOW DOES JESTER PERFORM IN THE BEDROOM?

More confident on the stage than he is on the mattress. If he's had a good performance on the former, you can expect something special on the latter.

WHAT IF JESTER IS YOUR PARTNER?

There must be times when you feel you are having to hold it all together, but in the end his compelling personality makes it worthwhile. Hope you like parties.

MOST LIKELY TO SAY

'Did you hear the one about the nun and the bishop?'

KEY QUESTION

What happens when you don't find his jokes funny any more? *Answer:* Turn up the volume on the TV or buy him a new joke book.

LIBMAN

Main characteristics

A pro-feminist male; politically correct; very well read; middle-class lefty; thoughtful, earnest, well intentioned, but rather intense.

What's he like?

In the early 1990s the media spotted a different type of man out on the streets. This man was a completely new species of male, never before seen outside select American university campuses. He was 'new man' and for many he came to represent a modern, enlightened era for males, one in which they showed how comfortable they were doing housework, changing nappies, demonstrating emotional intelligence – being very much like women in fact. Alas, new man proved to be a temporary phenomenon, for underneath all that new-found sensitivity towards women's issues there still lurked a male, loaded down with all the emotional baggage and masculine impulses that only males have. This proved to be something of a disappointment to all those women, especially feminists, who had hoped that their calls for change would eventually fall on receptive male ears. But new man has not entirely disappeared. He is still out there. It's just that he's a much more complicated character than was previously supposed. New man has transformed himself into Libman – the twenty-first century pro-feminist male who reads the *Guardian* or the *New York Times*, always votes Democrat or Labour, and makes sure his membership of Amnesty International and Greenpeace is paid up.

Libman first developed his sense of liberal maleness when he went to university and discovered that being mindlessly macho just didn't work with female sociology undergraduates. They got turned on by thoughtful and reflective intelligence rather than by drunken or laddish behaviour. Sure, in the end it led to the same thing, but at least he treated women as intellectual equals rather than as notches on a bedpost.

Since his undergraduate days and nights of intellectual and sexual discovery, mixed with a little recreational soft drug use, Libman has moved on. He is still decidedly respectable, but now rather frayed around the edges. All that heavy thinking has taken its toll. From being a bit of a campus radical in his youth, he is now comfortably ensconced among the greying middle-class élite that influences much of Western cultural and political life. Where once he could be found reading political sociologist Marcuse and playing air guitar to Led Zeppelin, he's now more inclined to the latest John Grisham thriller and Enya. He still smokes the occasional joint, but mainly so as to get off to sleep. His wardrobe has finally expanded from two pairs of blue jeans and a few T-shirts, but so has his waistline.

Can Libman be trusted in love?

On the whole, yes, you can trust Libman but you should be aware that this male face is a mix of contradictions. That may make him a particularly interesting male type to get involved with but, unfortunately, it also indicates that he often feels pulled in different directions. This is largely due to his desire to satisfy his 'needs' and his family's 'needs', and yet remain politically correct. For example, his liberal inclinations are to oppose globalisation but he likes his holidays in Goa and invariably succumbs to pressure from his kids to take them to Disney World. He recognises that cars are slowly but irrevocably destroying our environment, yet he and his wife couldn't possibly manage without their Toyota people carrier. He believes in the legalisation of drugs, but would be devastated if his own kids chased the dragon. He'd like to see the prisons emptied of most non-violent criminals, just so long as they didn't come and live near him. Although an avid supporter of equal opportunities, he can be surprisingly competitive and single-minded when it comes to protecting and promoting his own career. Importantly for future lovers, while Libman likes to see himself as sensitive to women's issues, which he is, there are occasions when sexual temptation can get the better of him.

Is Libman romantic?

Despite his liberal inclinations and flexible moral stance, this guy can be a little unsure of himself when it comes to romancing a woman. This unease is not borne of ambivalence over the relationship, rather it is just that he needs to loosen up a little and experiment. Similarly, he can be a bit uptight sexually, preferring the comfort of routine sex to the passion of something a little more illicit and dangerous. He's certainly not into the swinging scene and his eyes would pop if you came home one day with red crotchless panties and handcuffs, though secretly he'd be delighted.

Is Libman the marrying kind?

One of Libman's strengths is his loyalty coupled with a sense of what he would term 'social justice', so be confident that if you do get him down the aisle it'll be with love and commitment in his heart. However, this male face is often not for marrying. He sees marriage as establishment and dated, and much prefers to stay outside such an arrangement yet still in a regular partnership.

What sort of woman does Libman go for?

As will be obvious, Libman sees himself as a bit of a lefty. Indeed, some Libmen can be very political. This may range from regular meetings with Socialist Worker comrades to doorstepping for his party at election time, or just turning up at the occasional union meeting. He's not as prone to getting on his soapbox as Preacher is – he much prefers a quieter life. All this suggests that Libman goes for a woman who is very similar to himself – same middle-class expectations, same educational background, same professional status, same political views. Also, this is one of the few male faces who is comfortable living with a feminist. He is certainly no Neanderthal.

What is Libman like as a father?

In the UK there are now over 60,000 househusbands and the vast majority are Libmen – guys who have opted out of the corporate rat-race and decided to spend their time as full-time fathers and houseworkers. Libman takes fathering very seriously indeed and can make an excellent dad, although his liberal nature means that his kids can be rather rebellious. They'll probably grow up to be Libmen just like him.

As far as begetting kids is concerned, what you have with Libman is a guy who can generally produce the goods – all that jogging and a healthy diet means his sperm count is likely to be quite high. If that thought scares you off, be assured that this is one man you can trust to take the male pill. If the maternal instinct does strike and you both have the urge to fill the spare bedroom with something small and pink, wet and windy, not only will Libman attend the ante-natal classes, he'll likely massage you right through the birth.

Could you work for Libman?

Many Libmen decide that university life is altogether too comfortable to leave and stay on after getting their degrees, adding to their growing list of postgraduate qualifications, at the end of which they take up tenured posts as university lecturers. Alternatively, they may become such pillars of society as senior civil servants, media executives, political journalists, charity workers, health service managers or teachers. You are most likely to find Libman in those professions that are considered to be 'people centred'. Where you won't find him is in the armed forces, the police force, or as a director in the tobacco industry.

In general, then, this is one of the better male faces to work for. You won't have to argue your case for maternity leave and he'll even make sure his male employees take their equally important paternity leave. However, there is a side to Libman that can get drawn into all the management and organisational stuff, so watch for that. What happens is he suddenly finds, after several years at the chalk face, that he's now a middle or senior manager. He can then start acting like Corporate Man or Alpha Male, but in most cases it's just a passing phase.

Would you like Libman as a friend?

Yes, he makes a very solid friend – understanding, reliable and constant. Also, like Teddy Bear, Libman is comfortable with women purely as platonic friends – he is no skirt chaser in the way Romancer is.

Scientifically speaking

The French poststructuralist thinker Michel Foucault would likely have argued that Libman is very much an ungrounded discursive subject rooted in a multitude of signifying practices and languages, many of which have been largely influenced by feminism and feminist thinking emerging in Western society, and especially universities, during the past thirty years or so. Libman's sense of being male and masculine is acutely linked to the approving gaze of dominant, educated women. So it's no surprise that these are the types with whom he usually ends up having relationships.

Is Libman the man for you?

If you're the sort of woman who yearns for middle-class respectability, spiced up with a touch of the intellectual, Libman is your best bet among the male faces. I wouldn't rely on him always resisting sexual temptation, but he's no serial shagger. Given his educated background, he is unlikely to be out of work so he should be able to maintain a cosy lifestyle – for both your benefits. He has the potential to be a first rate househusband, and he won't feel at all threatened if you are Alpha Woman and heading for the top of the corporate heap.

His tendency to cynicism, ironic humour and earnestness may get some women down, especially those who like a man to be a little more earthy, streetwise and emotive. Also, Libman's tendency to snobbishness may not appeal to some. Despite their leftist leanings, Libmen are unmistakably middle class and if you don't feel middle class yourself it may be best to avoid this one. In the same vein, Libman is more likely to spend his evenings gardening, reading, or listening to Radio 4 than watching TV. As he sees it, *Big Brother* may be fine for the mindless masses but not for him. So what we have here is a predictable, slightly intense type of guy, someone who'd be quite happy to catch the odd outdoor concert by REM, but who is definitely past the clubbing stage of his life. This exemplar of modern masculinity, more comfortable in chinos than a suit, may seem boring to some but at least he cleans the loo.

Emotionally, unlike Alpha Male, Libman is riven with quite a lot of self-doubt, which could be the reason why he always likes to win an argument. In fact, he can be rather self-righteous and overbearing at times. More worryingly, Libmen have the capacity to use their intellect as a weapon in relationships, so watch out for that one. In his favour, he is thoughtful, gentle and will always listen to both points of view. He likes to think of himself as very democratic. He has the capacity to be emotionally mature but in a rather analytical way. In fact, quite a lot of Libmen can be very buttoned down with their emotions. They have a tendency to think and analyse, rather than just feel – not always a good thing in a relationship.

To sum up

Despite the numerous contradictions that trouble him, Libman is going to be around for a very long time. Across the world, universities are opening their doors to more and more young men and women who aspire to the comfortable lifestyle that Libman espouses. Not only is he educated, he is generally intelligent, resourceful and has the useful ability to be quite Machiavellian when it suits him. Some find their desire for financial security means they risk becoming a bit like Corporate Men, but most tend to plough their own independent furrows. So, on balance, we should welcome Libman to the male faces, not least because we need him as a counterweight to such males as Neanderthal and Rottweiler, who would quickly take us back into the dark ages if left unsupervised.

HOW TO SPOT A LIBMAN

You will certainly have met this man, most likely when you were at school or university. Perhaps he was your tutor – just maybe he was more than that.

HOW DOES LIBMAN PERFORM IN THE BEDROOM?

Got a lot of possibilities but you must get him to chill out a little first. Not very imaginative. Might help if you leave a copy of *The Sexual Life of Catherine M* lying around – a touch of cerebral sexuality.

WHAT IF LIBMAN IS YOUR PARTNER?

Don't always let him win the argument. Much as he might think so, he doesn't necessarily have all the answers.

MOST LIKELY TO SAY

'TV today is bloody rubbish.'

KEY QUESTION

Do you want to marry him?
Answer: Go ahead if you can live without ever again going to McDonald's, KFC or Starbucks.

MANCHILD

Main characteristics

Predatory male; expensive tastes; smooth and unctuous; smiles with a leer; an ageing stud, increasingly without dignity.

What's he like?

As women have long noted, many men never reach maturity, no matter how old they are. They seem forever rooted in a particular stage in their lives, still 'the lads', up for a laugh, out with their mates, chasing skirt, knocking back the pints, permanently engaged in holding middle-age at bay. Many male faces succumb to this pattern of behaviour, especially those who prefer the company of men to that of women. However, there is also a type of man who was once mature but who is now in reverse, his years and his dignity apparently tumbling away as quickly as his receding hairline. Such a one is Manchild.

A typical Manchild is likely to be over fifty, divorced, with several children, a fairly stable past but a very chequered future. He sees himself as smooth, saccharine sweet and a bit of a stud, but in fact he's in the middle of a very dangerous midlife crisis, which he attempts to stem by suddenly becoming incredibly shag-happy. Women are conquests, and he's about to have his share. He's usually in a comfortable job and, save for child maintenance costs, has a decent disposable income. He could well be running his own business, driving a flash company car, attired in a well-cut suit, and with a cottage in the country – one-bedroomed, of course – for those special weekends. Perhaps he's a well-known politician, respected and powerful, pontificating from his vantage point at the top of the parliamentary ladder. Maybe he's opted for early retirement and is filling his leisure hours by pursuing his new favourite pastime – women. Whatever his present situation, what is particularly interesting about Manchild is his past. You see, Manchild didn't start out as Manchild. He was an altogether different male face in his younger years, unlike Romancer, who exists primarily to capture and seduce.

Perhaps Manchild was an Alpha Male who came to grief in some bloody office coup, thereafter giving up the battle for corporate glory; or maybe he was Achilles, the man with it all but fatally flawed, his wife finally deciding, after a number of testing years, that she was not the one to save him from himself. He could have been Club Man, maybe still is a little, but became disillusioned with all that brotherhood stuff and decided that women's company wasn't so bad after all. Whatever his earlier incarnation, it set him up for being the Manchild he is today. It provided the foundations of his current character but in the process put him on a quite different path of masculinity. Now he is older, more urbane, but alas, not much wiser. He sees the future ahead but for him it spells out 'mortality'. It is this frantic attempt to stem the inevitable process of ageing that makes Manchild who he is, and it makes him dangerous.

Can Manchild be trusted in love?

Under no circumstances can you trust this man. He may be intelligent, successful and wealthy, but his behaviour in relationships borders on the pathological, especially for those unfortunate enough to fall in love with him.

Is Manchild romantic?

He may not be the best looking of men, but Manchild is one of the archetypal seducers among the male faces. He has romance and seduction down to a fine art. He is merciless in using his money and status to get access to women, especially younger more vulnerable ones, and he will blithely promise the earth in return for you agreeing to spend the weekend 'at my place in the Cotswolds'.

You may think that women would spot Manchild a mile off and avoid him at all costs. Well, you'd be wrong. Manchild has a lot to offer women and for every one who dismisses his lecherous overtures with a sneer, another will submit herself to his, and her, pleasure. She may well spot that this man carries more baggage than a jumbo jet, but she also knows that baggage can be interesting – Manchild is not a boring man to know. What's more, Manchild's extensive experience of life hasn't been entirely wasted and while much of his knowledge of women rests on simple assumptions and stereotypes, he has, over the years, built up quite an impressive stock of knowledge of women's wiles and ways. As he sees it, now is the time to put this knowledge to good effect.

He knows, for example, that women desire different things in their men, dependent on where they are in their lives at a particular time. Manchild has no illusions about his lack of attraction to those, usually younger, women seeking a long-term partner, marriage, children, home and security. But then, he's been down that road in the past and he'd no more return to that lifestyle than he would cut off the most precious and delicate part of him. So the fact that he doesn't give off signals as a potential home-loving mate bothers him not one iota. What he does know is that younger women may well be attracted to the material and sophisticated comforts he can offer – holidays in Bermuda, five-star country hotels, weekends in Vienna, à la carte dining. Similarly, he's well aware that while older women will initially be very wary of him, many will quite likely shelve their doubts in order to be with a man, maybe on a very casual basis, who knows how to press their special buttons when between the sheets. And anyway, Manchild has the skill of assuaging any woman's doubts by employing a tried and tested strategy for seduction – he doggedly persists with his flattering attentions, makes her feel wanted and desirable, and thereby encourages her to believe in the illusion that she is the one and only one for him. Even if she sees through all this scheming, she may well reckon it's worth the risk just to spice up her life. What she must not do, under any circumstances, is fall in love with Manchild. That would definitely be a risk too far.

Is Manchild the marrying kind?

Well, he certainly was in his previous incarnation as Uniform Man or Wallflower, but not any more. Should he ask you, and should you feel tempted to walk down the aisle with him, do make sure you have a strong get-out clause written into the contract.

What sort of woman does Manchild go for?

This male face has very eclectic tastes in women. Overall, younger women usually rate higher than older ones. The range of potential lovers available to Manchild is largely the result of his excellent knowledge of where to find women to add to his little black book of names. Some still prefer the traditional places for meeting potential lovers, such as nightclubs and the office – not the annual office party as he'll have spotted a target long before that comes round. Others are aware that Internet dating agencies and personal columns of newspapers open up a whole new world of opportunity. Many a Manchild adopts, over time, a particular tried and tested seductive strategy, one he tends to return to time and again. This might be the supermarket pick-up, where he approaches a woman on the pretext of appearing completely hopeless at shopping, asks for some advice, and immediately he's off into whatever spiel he's devised for situations like this. He could be the type who prefers to use cyberspace for his romantic moves, weaving his seductive magic via email, often winning his target's attention, if not heart, through his ability to stir sexual and romantic imaginings with carefully chosen phrases.

Okay, he's a bit of a bastard, but then he'd admit this himself. How he lives with such knowledge is his secret. To understand what drives him you have to remember that he's been and done all the long-termish marriage stuff and now he's up for short-term fun and frolics. He sees old age looming but he's damned if he's going to enter his dotage without a fight. Unlike many Romancers, with whom he otherwise has a lot in common, Manchild is unlikely to be in a steady relationship. He's going to be single and apparently available – which is one of the key baits in the love, or should I say sex, game he plays. Similarly, as he sees it, he's done respectability in his past life. Now he doesn't care what people think and, anyway, he knows that many men, especially those who are married, will be more than a little envious of his racy reputation. He also knows that many women will be more than a little curious about what makes him tick.

What is Manchild like as a father?

If his kids are still talking to him, it's usually a good indicator that Manchild has managed his parenting role with some success.

Could you work for Manchild?

You probably have done at some point in your life. Did you spot him among all the other male faces? Perhaps you succumbed to his particular charms. More likely, you watched from a distance, both amused and bemused at your boss going through a fully-fledged midlife crisis.

Would you like Manchild as a friend?

When he's not devoting his time and attention to sexual pursuits, Manchild is probably to be found with his mates, most of whom will also be Manchildren. They make a pretty interesting spectacle when they are all out together, a pack of ageing studs, cavalier and thin on top, speeding to some casino or restaurant in their sportscars. As with Cool Poser, this is not a man you'll find on the bus. They'll be dressed to kill, their designer clothes carefully selected for the occasion or venue. Again like Cool Poser, even when he's dressing down, Manchild looks as though he's spent hours carefully ensuring that his casualness is subtly effective and flattering.

Scientifically speaking

The sort of behaviour that Manchild exhibits is sometimes diagnosed as a condition of the male menopause and is often related to a hormonal decline of testosterone. In psychological terms,

Manchild's extreme change of lifestyle and behaviour, from good boy to bad boy, can be understood as a midlife crisis, a crisis of masculinity, or even a condition of temporary insanity. However the experts describe it, Manchild's behaviour carries many risks for those who get involved with him.

Is Manchild the man for you?

Only if you are a masochist, hopelessly in love with him, or an eternal optimist.

However, despite the fact that this is a dangerous face to love and that he's a user of women, Manchild can himself be used. He may think that he's clever and suave, but he can't help giving off those danger signals by being a little oily, slick and unctuous. So if you do find yourself involved with Manchild, my advice is to play him at his own game. As I say, don't fall in love. He's never going to be faithful. He's always going to play away. Importantly, you'll never be able to believe him when he's lying next to you, his hand artfully caressing your beauty spots, and he whispers, 'I've waited for you all my life. I've never met a woman like you. I love you so much.' You can, however, believe him when he's lying exhausted afterwards and mutters, 'God, that was good.' It might well have been equally good for you too.

To sum up

What you have with Manchild is someone who will promise women the earth but deliver only disappointment. He's a man who knows how to treat a woman, both in and out of bed, and he'll also have a well-tuned, if rather stereotypical, sense of the feminine mind. But despite all this, he is a man in fear – of old age, his declining sexual prowess possibly propped up by Viagra, and his growing paunch. As the years go by so his search for that increasingly elusive youthfulness becomes more acute and desperate. Designer clothes, good restaurants, fine wine and expensive cars are all very well, but they really don't compare to the one thing that truly inflates this man's sense of his masculinity – a beautiful young woman on his arm. In fact, for him, the young is more important than the beautiful, for he gets a special kick from dominating and controlling less experienced and more innocent minds. But whomever he attracts, and he always attracts someone, no one woman can satisfy him any more. The big loves in his life have come and gone. Now he's on the prowl, eager to fill his final decades with lively lust and lechery. A sophisticated predator, camouflaged and fast moving, Manchild inhabits many parts of the social jungle. Enjoy the ride on this ageing tiger but have your exit at hand.

HOW TO SPOT A MANCHILD

If you are looking for this type of guy, put your profile on an Internet dating agency site. You'll have to sift through a lot of Zebedees and Trainspotters, but he'll turn up eventually. If you don't want to meet this type of guy, stay indoors and watch TV.

HOW DOES MANCHILD PERFORM IN THE BEDROOM?

A highly sexual guy – just make sure he's got his Viagra to hand as his desires often exceed his capabilities. Probably got an extensive collection of porn videos for added stimulation. Very open-minded – hope you are.

WHAT IF MANCHILD IS YOUR PARTNER?

You have my sympathy. You know it's way too late for marriage guidance, so what keeps you in the game? Maybe you don't want to risk ending up with Neanderthal.

MOST LIKELY TO SAY

'It's raining so why walk? My Porsche is right outside.'

KEY QUESTION

When he takes you back to his bachelor pad, which of these magazines is 'carelessly' left on the coffee table for you to see – *Erotic Review*, *Loaded* or *Lancashire Life?*

Answer: All three. He'll carefully observe which one you pick up to read.

MR ANGRY

Main characteristics

Very unpredictable; fundamentally frustrated; argumentative and aggressive; doesn't recognise his behaviour is damaging; his mood swings are the only certainty.

What's he like?

Most of us have a temper. Most of us have an invisible line, the crossing of which takes us into a whole new territory of our personality, and it's not a nice place to be. This is our dark side, an aspect we prefer to keep hidden from polite company, that bit of ourselves that lurks in the nether regions of our brain, rarely surfacing. As with the Hulk, it can be triggered at particular times of stress and frustration, but for most of us it remains submarine, below the otherwise calm seas of our character. We might blow now and again, but it's a very unusual occurrence for we have learnt to control our more explosive feelings and emotions if we want to keep our jobs, our friends and our marriages. We save our explosions for the 'big ones', the fights that really matter, Armageddon. Well, most of us do. For a few of us, the 'big ones' seem to come round with disturbing regularity. For such men, titanic conflict perpetually hovers around them in a black, heavy, thunderous cloud.

These are Mr Angries and while they may well be one male face we'd probably like to see less of, they are never far away. They jostle us on the tube, try to barge in at the taxi rank and stand fuming behind us in the bus queue. Yet despite this unsettling, distinctly unsociable side to his character, Mr Angry is quite a contradictory person. He can be a loving husband, father, partner. He can be kind, considerate and faithful, gentle and thoughtful. He can be a hardworking professional. He can be a loyal and attentive friend. It's just that he has this one problem – his anger. Mr Angry has a short fuse and it gets lit very quickly. Once he blows, watch out.

In times of old, Mr Angry would likely have been enlisted into the army to fight for king and country, and he'd have been very welcome among the troops, just the sort of bloke you want beside you when the enemy's bearing down. He'd stand his ground, seething with anger and determined to wipe the foe from the face of the earth. Sure, he'd be constantly getting into trouble with his sergeant, but come the day, Mr Angry would be your rock. Today, Mr Angries are still to be found in the armed forces and similar brotherhoods of men, but in the modern army there is less call for his particular skills. He's had to relocate to more genteel professions, anything in fact that pays a living wage. He could be the guy who sets off on the commuter trail every morning at 8.30, he could be the bus driver who stops to pick him up, or maybe he's the builder working on the new roundabout at the bottom of your road. He's there, but difficult to spot. Mr Angry may have a temper like no other man, but don't expect to see signs of this in his appearance. Okay, he may have high blood pressure and a slightly ruddy complexion as a result, but otherwise he looks like everyman.

A Mr Angry I once knew used to run his own business. He was a devoted workaholic, getting up at around 5.00 a.m. six days a week and working through to 6.00 p.m. or later. He rarely took a break or a holiday. He owned a couple of shops and you'd think his people skills would be pretty good, but not at all. Stalin had more people skills than this guy. When you walked in his shop, he had the knack of making you feel guilty about being there, as if he was saying, 'So you're here again. What do you want? Can't you see I'm busy!' Customers were an irritant and intrusion to this Mr Angry. As far as he was concerned, customer relations skills were a foreign language. You might ask why I bothered going back to his shop. Well, I found it both fascinating and slightly amusing to see him getting flustered and frustrated over the merest problem. Maybe he couldn't find a particular product, or the electronic till had broken down, or one of his staff hadn't turned up that day. Whatever his problem, it quickly stressed him out and that was bad news – for him and everyone around him.

Can Mr Angry be trusted in love?

You can trust him in love, but not in his less intimate human relationships. Also, be aware that he has a jealous side, so for him the relevant question is can he trust you? Contradictions in his character constantly arise to cause problems for him in his life. For example, he can be a dedicated father, but if his teenaged daughter comes home late at night once too often, all fuses blow. He may love his wife dearly, but his inherent jealousy inevitably rises to the surface now and again, especially if she's of an independent mind, as increasing numbers of women are. Quick to anger, he is often at loggerheads with someone, whether it be the local pub landlord, a member of the family, a neighbour or his boss. He can go to work in the morning calm and relaxed, and return at night a fuming volcano ready to burst. Trust him not to stray. Don't trust him to give you a quiet life.

Is Mr Angry romantic?

Despite his urgent need for an anger management course, many women consider Mr Angry to have some good things going for him, not least his traditional views about love and romance. He is quite good at making a woman feel important and remembering flowers, birthdays, anniversaries and the roses on Valentine's Day. Women can also be attracted to what appears to be his inner strength, and then become even more fascinated at the weakness it conceals. Those who set up home with this guy come to recognise that while Mr Angry may be a bit of a loner, at the day's end he needs the warmth and comfort of his home and family. This is the only place he truly relaxes. This is the bait that attracts some women to Mr Angry – they end up protecting him from himself, mothering him. They provide him with the safety of a nest from where he can shut out the rest of the world, or shout at it.

Is Mr Angry the marrying kind?

Yes. For Mr Angry marriage is the most natural state between men and women and he's often quite intolerant of more casual relationships. He is quite patriarchal in his attitudes; marriage is, for him, also about ownership and dominance in a relationship. Women who are married to Mr Angries have to be almost saint-like to tolerate his sometimes aggressive mood swings. Any woman who has been married to him for several years is likely to be quite skilled at spotting coming eruptions, and their causes, before they get out of hand. That is not so surprising because she has to be his very opposite if the relationship is to survive his self-destruct tendencies. If she was as prone to anger as he is, life would be just impossible. But despite this, don't expect to find Mr Angry down at the singles club on a Friday night, trying his hand, or feet, at salsa or the foxtrot, polishing his chat-up lines. One of the most interesting things about this guy is that he usually has a woman in his life.

What sort of woman does Mr Angry go for?

Certainly not a feminist or any woman with a strong sense of independence and a desire to carve her own niche in the world. He is most comfortable with more traditionally minded women, those who are prepared to sacrifice their own wants and needs for his. He is also completely emotionally illiterate and lacking the ability to reflect on his actions, so he's not going to stay long with any woman who keeps pointing that fact out to him.

What is Mr Angry like as a father?

He can make a devoted dad, but his narrow mindset, traditional gender values and short fuse do not make for a quiet home life. His children are likely to stay out of his way when they are young but from age thirteen or so onwards, life can be very fraught for everyone. This is when his teenaged son or daughter will start to challenge his authority as a father and patriarch.

Could you work for Mr Angry?

As you might guess, this is not one of the best faces to work for. He's the last guy you want to be chairing a politically sensitive meeting. You don't want him as the boss of anything large and complex, nor as leader of any union – he just couldn't handle the delicate negotiations with the bosses. You don't want him in any position of responsibility that demands careful considered attention to detail, and you certainly don't want him working in counselling or customer relations. He's best when he's working on his own, to his own timetable, independent and not reliant on others. In short, he's not much use in a team unless you want someone there to scare the others.

Would you like Mr Angry as a friend?

Mr Angry often makes a better friend than he does neighbour, the reason being he can choose his mates but not his neighbours. For example, in a neighbourhood where I once lived, two Mr Angries came to blows over a hedge that separated their houses. It was a small, insignificant hedge, a quiet, tidy hedge that had been there for many years until the two Mr Angries moved in and took ownership of it. Well, they each thought they had ownership of it and that was the problem. Neither would give way, neither would consider compromising for the sake of peace. Both wanted victory. It went on like that for years until one night one of the Mr Angries lost it completely and destroyed the hedge in a paraffin fireball.

Scientifically speaking

Men's propensity for aggression and anger is often put down to them having a higher level of testosterone than females. However, such ideas only serve to reinforce the myth that male behaviour is rooted in biology rather than culture. If we follow this line of thinking, Mr Angry is destined always to be, well, angry. By contrast, Irish psychiatrist Anthony Clare notes that the relationship between testosterone and male aggression is much more complex than simple biological theories would suggest. We know, for instance, that young boys can be aggressive and yet have very low levels of testosterone. We also know that not all men are aggressive, despite having similar if not identical levels of the male sex hormone. To understand what makes Mr Angry tick we have to go beyond biology and into the particular conditions and attitudes that sustain dominant masculine cultures. Mr Angry can unlearn his behaviour, but only if he decides to do so.

Is Mr Angry the man for you?

While he may appear to many women something of a nightmare partner, Mr Angry is not inherently unlikeable. He can be quite sociable and amenable when the mood takes him, but there is always this side to his character which eventually gets in the way of his relationships. However, if you asked him, Mr Angry would say that he is a very calm and reasonable guy – it's just that other people get him mad, make him annoyed. This may be true to a point, and we all get angry at some things, but only the Mr Angries of this world have a volcanic nature, always just about to blow, steam coming out of their ears, fuming with indignation at something or someone.

Mr Angry is clearly an unstable character. He may even be physically aggressive, and certainly up for an argument if he's challenged. Much of this conflict stems from wanting the world around him to be perfect – but it never is. Most of us get used to the imperfections around us, but not Mr Angry. He sees imperfection, in himself and other people, as something intolerable. He cannot abide it. Given this, you'd think that he'd stay away from those 'hot topics' – religion and politics – but not so. Mr Angry has the knack of being able to articulate his opinions but only up to a point. When that point is reached, intellectual and reasoned argument comes to a complete halt and something much more primitive and basic takes over.

However, while you may find him in the bar now and again, discussing politics with his few mates, remember that most Mr Angries are home birds. They are a very sad species when they are angry and alone. If you are the one to rescue this man from his intemperate moods, to calm him down and unstress him, hitch up with him because he will always need you, and he'll love you for it. Just don't expect a peaceful life in return.

To sum up

Look out for a Basil Fawlty character, a frustrated, perfection-seeking, hot-tempered idealist, a man with strongly held political or religious beliefs, but with only limited verbal skills. If you have none of these weaknesses, perhaps it could work. The question is, is it worth the effort?

HOW TO SPOT A MR ANGRY

Listen for someone who shouts a lot and seems to be in a hurry. May well drive a white van – very fast.

HOW DOES MR ANGRY PERFORM IN THE BEDROOM?

Can be quite into sex – needs it to relax. Won't take kindly to suggestions that he might be under-performing so go gentle with him at first. Likes to dominate.

WHAT IF MR ANGRY IS YOUR PARTNER?

You should go into marriage guidance – as a counsellor. After all these years of living with your Mr Angry, I would bet you're an expert at defusing tempers and heated situations.

MOST LIKELY TO SAY

'What! You can't be serious!'

KEY QUESTION

You are on a blind date and you suspect you've ended up with a Mr Angry. How do you know for sure?
Answer: Find out his political beliefs and engage him in argument.

MURDOCH

Main characteristics:

A driven man; relentless and untiring; loves tax havens; quite ruthless; has Napoleonic self-belief – usually justified.

What's he like?

The Romans hailed him as Caesar, the Huns knew him as Attila, the Zulus feared him as Shaka. For us, he is Murdoch, the archetypal empire builder. Named after one of the richest and most powerful men on this planet, a man with a worldwide media empire, Murdoch is the ultimate twenty-first century competitor – aggressive, cold, audacious, ruthless, clever and totally focused.

Of all the male faces, Murdoch is one of the most fascinating. What makes Murdochs what they are? What drives their unlimited ambition? What goes on in their heads? What goes on in their beds? These questions have spawned endless books, informed thousands of earnest biographies and fuelled countless myths and sagas. We remain endlessly fascinated by Murdoch's character, whether it be found in Henry V, Napoleon, Henry Ford, Genghis Khan, Alexander the Great or Hitler. We ordinary mortals can never get enough of these men, for they simultaneously fascinate us yet repel us. Their deeds and exploits are the stuff of legend, and that is the way most of us know them and relate to them – at a distance, through the cinema screen and storybooks. We are like moths to their flame, always wanting to find out more about the men who rise to lead us, threaten to terrorise us and fill us with hope and fear. We may worship them, we may loathe them – we cannot ignore them. They may be touched by Zeus himself, but who would want one for a father? Who would even want one for a neighbour?

Murdochs have always been with us. Since the beginnings of time, Murdochs have periodically surfaced in different cultures, different countries, often from quite lowly, insignificant beginnings. From being the small boy tending sheep on the hillside, Murdochs have gone on to build armies, cutting swathes of hope and terror across their world. From being the bookish college student, Murdochs have transformed themselves into men who built commercial empires – and crushed others in the process. From inauspicious beginnings in petty crime, Murdochs have become legendary Godfathers. Yet while Murdochs may be household names worldwide, it's unlikely you have ever met one, or ever will, for this is the most elusive, the most elevated of male faces. Even if you work for him, or follow him in his army, you will rarely meet Murdoch face to face. He lives a rarefied existence, surrounded by his immediate family, his courtiers, his closest allies. He parties only when it suits his strategy to do so, he makes friends only with those who can help him in his ambitions, he loves himself above all others. Ultimately, he relies only on his own judgement. Most importantly, he trusts only himself.

It is no surprise, then, to know that Murdoch is a user of people. He would be, wouldn't he? This is no gentleman. He's not to be found teaching in a primary school. He'd make an appalling social worker. No, this is a man with clear intent and unambiguous aims in life – to be the very, very best. More than that, he wants to go down in history. He is much more interested in how he will be remembered than in how he will be loved. In pursuit of this aim, Murdoch comes to measure all those around him by one criterion – 'Can I use them, and if so how?' This highly intelligent, self-made man may have somewhat limited emotional understanding, but his heart throbs with unresolved desire for greater and greater glories. His ambition knows no limits. His manipulative skill together with his Machiavellian instinct and often charming exterior, provide a powerful if not irresistible combination of forces for him to draw on in his quest for glory. How can we resist such a man? Well, for the most part we cannot. We have to accept that Murdochs will always be around. We may come to detest them or we may worship them, but it seems we cannot live without them. They are men who make history, often in their own image. Their brutality can be horrendous, their passion for glory can be grotesque, yet there is something about Murdochs that attracts us to them. We march for them, sweat for them, run from them.

Despite their omnipresence in our lives, Murdochs are, I guess, cursed. These men cannot ever walk the streets like ordinary mortals. They can never fully trust those who flatter them, or seek to befriend or love them. Often surrounded by jealous sycophants, and bodyguards, Murdochs are compelled to live in a hyper-real, twilight world of their own making. Tragically, many live to see their empires crumble in the end – all those five-year plans, all those memos and emails, gone to dust.

Can Murdoch be trusted in love?

Trust is a word that Murdoch will utter constantly, usually in the context of his employees and those with whom he does business although, for him, trust is often an elusive concept. You can, however, trust him to safeguard and protect his interests. If that includes you, then you should be okay.

Is Murdoch romantic?

Romance is something to which Murdoch gives a lot of time and thought. He is a larger than life male and so will be inclined to give larger than life gifts and surprises. Expect the very best hotels in the most exclusive locations, arriving there in a private aeroplane. Many Murdochs actually own islands in the sun. Where better for enjoying those long lingering nights together?

Is Murdoch the marrying kind?

Straight Murdochs rarely remain single for long. There is inevitably some woman who will capture their hearts if not their wallets. Murdoch is, however, ambivalent about the state of marriage. He can take it or leave it. It is usually his lover who insists on the legalising of the arrangement, for reasons that might be obvious. However, don't pursue Murdoch with one eye on the divorce settlement if it all goes pear-shaped. Whatever settlement you managed to get would be entirely up to him. His lawyers and accountants would make sure you got sweet zero if it suited him. On the other hand, Murdoch can be ever so generous with his family, if only because his children are, for him, the heirs to his empire.

What sort of woman does Murdoch go for?

This man loves the beautiful, the special, the sophisticated and the untouchably elegant. No woman is too far up the social ladder for him. He goes for women who add to his aura rather than detract from it. Murdoch is a very sexual male. All that phallic symbolism with which he surrounds himself – big cars, big houses, tower blocks – eventually transfers itself to his more intimate part – his brain. Consequently, Murdoch finds his sexual libido rises and falls with his corporation's share price. It should come as no surprise that Murdochs have a strong sexual attraction for women, and, if they so desire, for men also. Murdochs will only sleep alone if that is their preference. Otherwise, there will inevitably be a disciple or follower only too willing to pleasure his or her master, to be the body to provide warmth and much more through the long night. Sexual attraction is never simple and it is rarely just about looks. Indeed, Murdoch may be a very poor physical specimen himself – jowly, overweight, troubled with gout – but that matters not a jot. Murdoch has something much more potent, much more captivating to offer in the game of seduction – he has power.

As many women who have been loved by a Murdoch come to know, power has an interesting capacity to transfer itself. She may be no Murdoch herself, her ambition may extend no further than providing him with his necessary heirs, but the wife of Murdoch can expect to take her place up there amongst the élite, privileged, wealthy, protected. His sun shines on her and in the process she prospers, as do her children. So long as her husband's star holds sway, she can rule as a queen. But if the thought of being a Mrs Murdoch sends you into uncontrollable delight, tread carefully. It is a long and dangerous road to that end. The paths of Murdochs are littered with wannabe wives. This is a man with the capacity for love but with an even greater capacity for being callous and unsparing when he chooses.

What is Murdoch like as a father?

Fathering children will, for Murdoch, be just another public sign of his power and potency. This is especially so in the case of boys as they will be the ones he'll most likely expect to join him at the top of his empire. In all other respects, parenting is not one of his strong points. You can, however, rely on him to pay for the most exclusive and professional nannies, so you shouldn't have to change nappies unless you want to.

Could you work for Murdoch?

Few people work for Murdoch directly as he's very choosy about whom he allows into his inner sanctum. If you do happen to find yourself in that place, you'll certainly be very highly paid, which is some compensation for the demands he'll make of you. However, millions of us work for a Murdoch indirectly for the simple reason that he and his type own much of the infrastructure that drives the modern global capitalist economy. While Murdoch hates following rules, preferring to make his own, he'll certainly expect employees to follow his rules fastidiously.

Would you like Murdoch as a friend?

Of course you would! Just think of all those weeks on his island in the sun, or the occasional free flight in his Lear jet to the South of France, although if you are that close to him it's more than likely that you own your own island and Lear jet. He is close only to those whom he considers his equals, and there aren't many of them.

Scientifically speaking

Much masculinity is grounded in myth, and, as philosopher Roland Barthes noted, myths are dangerous because they appear so real while in fact they 'deprive the object of all history'. We come to believe the myth but in so doing lose a sense of what exists behind it and sustains it. This is the situation with Murdoch. He is engaged in an heroic project, building his empire. In the process, myths surround the man and come to be the man himself. As much as anything, it is this pursuit of myth that drives Murdoch, for he rightly knows it is his myth that will carry over into history long after he is with his god.

Is Murdoch the man for you?

Do not pursue this particular male face unless you too have that special something, that deep essence of self-protection combined with just a smattering of Murdoch's unbridled ambition. Like your paramour, you should be prepared to keep all-comers at bay. Importantly, you should have no hesitation in dispatching to the gallows any who would be queen. In his world, compassion is an expendable emotion. So it must be in yours if you are to survive.

Not only must you be implacable towards your sexual competitors, you must be forgiving to your man. Murdoch is one male face who is not for turning. He is never, ever going to be another male face. He is what he is and will remain so for all his days. Love him with this knowledge at the forefront of your mind. Your forgiveness of Murdoch must know no bounds. Accept that there will be times when he'll be unfaithful, he will have his mistresses, and he may even love another. But so long as he returns to your bed you have him. Do not, under any circumstances, attempt to dictate to this man, to control him. He may allow you some leeway to be his conscience at times, and he'll even perversely welcome you scolding him when he goes too far in his thoughtless treatment of others, but there will be limits. Go beyond them at your peril.

To sum up

Whether he wears a cardigan, a uniform or a suit, Murdoch should never be underestimated. His attraction for women is undeniable, but don't work for him unless you are willing to subsume your life to his needs and wishes. Don't marry him unless you are prepared to be mistress to his ego. Don't love him unconditionally, because he can never return that level of love to you. If you do dare tangle with Murdoch, be prepared for the ride of your life, to the stars and back. But remember, he never stops, he never eases down, he has an empire to build, and too short a life in which to do it.

HOW TO SPOT A MURDOCH

Just go down to your local bookshop – there's bound to be biographies of several of them. If you want to meet one in the flesh, start by circulating among the rich and famous.

HOW DOES MURDOCH PERFORM IN THE BEDROOM?

Many Murdochs are blessed with a sexual libido and energy almost as big as their ego. However, his Olympian work ethic and lack of exercise means that Murdoch will flag as much as he'll flagpole, although many Murdochs sire children well into their dotage. Power – what an aphrodisiac!

WHAT IF MURDOCH IS YOUR PARTNER?

What a story you must be able to tell but it's unlikely ever to be published as I bet you had to sign a confidentiality clause a couple of days before the wedding.

MOST LIKELY TO SAY

'Get me my accountants, now!'

KEY QUESTION

When was the last time he had a full eight hours sleep? And when he tries to get off to sleep at night, what does he count – sheep or his bank accounts?

Answer: He is a five hours a night man (sleep that is), and his preferred bedtime reading is his latest profit and loss sheet.

NEANDERTHAL

Main characteristics

Anti-feminist; very traditional male; outdated views on women and relationships; family man so long as he's in control.

What's he like?

The most profound revolution of the twentieth century was neither the Russian nor Chinese – it was the gender one. Inspired by feminists and feminisms, this revolution in women's attitudes and expectations has outlasted either of the other two and has affected countless men and women worldwide, and it's still going on. Indeed, some theorists claim that the rise in religious fundamentalism is, in part, an attempt by traditionally minded men to stem or roll back the gender revolution – to put women back in the home. So while feminism may have become an uncool word for many, the message it carries continues to inspire millions of women to strive for financial, sexual and emotional independence.

Not surprisingly, like all revolutions, the gender one has its supporters and its detractors. We can see among the male faces which ones are comfortable with women's independence and which are not. Libman, Backpacker, Teddy Bear and Achilles, while very different faces, each in their own way exhibit a modern form of masculinity that doesn't feel threatened by strong-minded women and their presence in politics, management and the professions. More male faces will have to come to terms with the implications of the gender revolution.

The data speaks for itself. In the US, over one third of all married women earn more than their husbands. In the UK, females are outperforming males on every educational indicator, and now account for over half the working population. Across the world, millions more women are becoming educated and, as a consequence, financially independent of men. From Jamaica to Japan, women in increasing numbers are choosing cohabitation and singledom over marriage, and if they choose to have children at all, it's later in life and fewer of them. In China, hitherto a very male dominated and traditional society, there has been a veritable explosion in the number of divorces, now exceeding two million a year, mostly instigated by women. Recent research in the UK, Australasia, the US and the Far East, shows that women of all ages and cultures are changing their sexual behaviour and increasingly indulging in serial relationships rather than making a lifetime commitment to one man. Not surprisingly, women are becoming increasingly impatient with those male faces who want to stem the gender tide. Such a man is Neanderthal.

This name was suggested to me by several of the women I interviewed for this book. To them, he is a typical hater of women, an avid anti-feminist and someone who, over many years, has bottled up an intense dislike of what he refers to as 'women's libbers'. Neanderthals are to be found anywhere there are men. They can be middle-aged, working-class labourers on a building site, or young money brokers earning fortunes in the city. They may be in the uniformed services, paying lip-service to equal opportunities policies, or they could be the sad single 'geezer' still living with his mum who gets his self-esteem from the branded goods he spends his salary on.

Some Neanderthals take their dislike of women's lib to extremes, getting actively involved in anti-feminist movements. Such men can be found in the UK Men's Movement and may well be readers or contributors to the Internet website www.ihatefeminists.com. In America, many Neanderthals are signed-up members of the Christian Promise Keepers movement. You often see gangs of Neanderthals out on the streets of European cities, usually in fascist mode, sporting right-wing regalia and mouthing obscenities at those who don't share their extreme views. Whatever country they are from, Neanderthals want the same thing – they want change. They are not at all happy with the current trend towards equal opportunities for women, seeing it as disrupting men's mythical inner essence, leaving them marginalised and in crisis. In other words, Neanderthals dream of a time when women surrender to men's natural superiority, return to the kitchen and leave men in power as the family breadwinners and decision makers. Some chance!

Can Neanderthal be trusted in love?

The Christian Promise Keepers do promise to love, honour and cherish their wives at all times. They promise to be faithful unto death and never to stray. In return, they expect their wives to be submissive homemakers. They are also anti-gay and anti-lesbian. Why can't these men just do the faithful bit without having to insist on their wives surrendering to them as a condition of their fidelity?

Is Neanderthal romantic?

In his own limited way, Neanderthal has the capacity to be quite romantic. In fact, he will expect to take the lead in romance, so if you are the sort of woman who likes to surprise her partner with weekends in Rome or Prague, or buys him flowers for his birthday, maybe he's not for you. If you want to make him feel really good about himself, allow Neanderthal to make the running in the game of love and romance. Be passive and demure, look up to him, ask his advice, make him feel important and let him make all the decisions. If you can't do that, at least let it seem to him that he's making all the decisions.

Is Neanderthal the marrying kind?

For some Neanderthals, marriage is the key to their identity. It is through the established order and structure of marriage that they get to feel like proper men. Marriage gives them, and their wives, a clear set of rules and guidelines to follow, underpinned as it is by laws and religious ideology. Neanderthals are astute enough to recognise that marriage has traditionally favoured men over women. In its more fundamentalist interpretation, marriage places very strong conditions on women, mainly through home and childcare responsibilities, while leaving men free to make their mark in the world of work. Good examples of this are the male Mormons who somehow manage to interpret the bible so as to prove they can have several wives, but their wives only one husband. So Neanderthals support marriage so long as they are in control of it. Similarly, they are very much against divorce, especially if it's instigated by their wives and not by them. Marry a Neanderthal and one way or another you've got him for keeps.

What sort of woman does Neanderthal go for?

One of the difficulties for Neanderthal is that he tends to relate to women as stereotypes of femininity – typically, either

Madonna or whore syndrome. Young Neanderthals may find it hard to form lasting relationships with women. They may be angry at having a woman as their boss, or they may just be a little sex starved. Older Neanderthals, especially if they've gone through a messy divorce, are unemployed or in work that they consider below them, can be very angry men and are best avoided by more sensitive souls. Much of their inner anger, while directed at modern woman, can be dissipated by a loving and patient wife or partner – if he can find one – but Neanderthal does get a good feeling from having something, and someone, to blame for his predicament.

What is Neanderthal like as a father?

Fatherhood can be a really big issue for Neanderthals. It is one of those areas of life that can assume strong political dimensions – especially when things go wrong in the marriage. Many Neanderthals are dispossessed dads who have, as they see it, lost out in the battle for custody of their children after divorce. They feel hard done by, accusing the courts and judges of treating them as 'second-class citizens', men with 'fewer rights than terrorists'. There are, of course, many sides to complex custody battles, but Neanderthals fail to see that if there is a bias in society towards mothers looking after their children, it's come about through bitter experience of most men's lack of interest in the practical side of childcare. For example, a recent UK study of 19,000 babies born in 2000 and 2001 found that more than a quarter of their fathers had never changed a nappy. Many of these dads will be Neanderthals – men who may well talk a good talk as hands-on dads and heads of their families, but who actually leave their wives to do the dirty work.

Could you work for Neanderthal?

If you are his mate you may not be too troubled by Neanderthal's narrow mind. You may well find his sexist jokes okay and not be overly concerned at the few women he promotes to positions of responsibility in the organisation. If you are a woman, especially a women who wants to climb the career ladder, the attitudes and practices in which Neanderthal engages will anger you very much indeed. As you come to know him better, you may well ponder where this dinosaur has come from and why he's not been put out to grass. You will find it reprehensible that so few women make it to the board of the company while men such as he seem to prosper. Keep fighting. His days are numbered only he doesn't know it yet.

Would you like Neanderthal as a friend?

This is one of the male faces who can appear a real 'man's man', one of the lads, a good geezer. Go to any pub, wine bar or nightclub on a weekend and you'll see young and not-so-young Neanderthals at leisure with their mates. It's a fascinating sight watching Neanderthal assume the position he knows best – pub pundit. He's an expert on everything, or so he thinks, and after a few pints he's not inclined to tolerate dissent, and certainly not from any women who may be around. If this is your type of guy, by all means join him at the bar. If not, best stay away as he's there to pontificate, not to exchange rational and considered points of view.

Scientifically speaking

American feminist Susan Faludi has explored the notion of 'masculinity in crisis'. This idea arises from studies that reveal the large numbers of men failing to respond positively to the massive social, cultural and economic upheavals of the twentieth century. Gender identity is central to these changes, influencing our core being, though we may live it out in individual ways. For those men who hold on to outdated notions of masculinity, the changes wrought by the gender revolution can appear extremely threatening. One way many such men attempt to deal with this predicament is to retreat into misogynistic attitudes and overt hostility towards women, although this serves only to marginalise them further. Neanderthal is such a man.

Is Neanderthal the man for you?

I hope some women are prepared to take this guy on, because unless they do he's destined for a pretty miserable time – angry, embittered, frustrated and yet blissfully unaware and ignorant of the fact that his sexist attitude in any way contributes to his plight. However, from the interviews I've undertaken with women for this book, it would seem Neanderthal is likely to be heading the way of the dodo – and sooner than he thinks.

To sum up

Do not mistake Neanderthal's outdated misogynism as indicative of his intelligence. He is not stupid. He can be very clever and resourceful and will often try to back up his arguments with pop-psychology theories. What he is is a traditional conservative who is well past his sell-by date but doesn't yet realise it. Neanderthal deserves his name because he is really a throwback to an earlier time, a period in history when men ruled both the home and the workplace, unchallenged in either domain by educated, intelligent females. Thankfully, such days are rapidly becoming history. Consequently, this male face is one whose future looks decidedly uncertain. In fact, he could well be on his way to becoming an extinct species. Until then, we will have to accept that there are still many Neanderthals out there. Some can be re-educated out of their narrow views; for others, there is no hope.

HOW TO SPOT A NEANDERTHAL

Could be any man. If unsure, ask him his views on women's lib.

HOW DOES NEANDERTHAL
PERFORM IN THE BEDROOM?

As one woman I interviewed put it, 'With Neanderthals, you have to switch off your brain for them to get an erection.'

WHAT IF NEANDERTHAL IS YOUR PARTNER?

I hope you don't have to switch off your brain too often.

MOST LIKELY TO SAY

'Why are men so badly treated today?'

KEY QUESTION

What book should you buy him for his birthday?
Answer: If you want to impress him, buy *Iron John* by Robert Bly. If you want him to learn something about modern man, buy him *The Politics of Manhood* by Michael Kimmel.

PREACHER

Main characteristics

Political animal; fundamentalist views; single-minded in his beliefs; fervent and intense; always on a mission.

What's he like?

For most of us, politics is something we steer away from. It's altogether too confusing if not boring. Anyway, aren't politicians all the same, worse than estate agents and lawyers, not to be trusted? If this is what you believe, you are unlikely to get turned on by this male type. His name is Preacher and he's one very committed guy – committed, that is, to his strongly held beliefs. Sure, we all have opinions and views but this male face holds them close to his heart. For him, his life is no less than a mission to change the world. As he sees it, he believes in his vision, so why shouldn't the rest of us?

Preacher is most comfortable when pontificating from the pulpit, haranguing from the soapbox or lecturing from the lectern. He is least comfortable having to listen to someone else's views, especially if they oppose his own. He loves an argument, not just to win it but to get the chance to make his case for the perfect world, for this man believes in Utopia, which is nice.

But the Utopia he offers is, alas, always just around the corner, or in the afterlife, never in the here and now. This absence of a practical and immediate example of what Preacher's world might look like should we give him half the chance to create it, makes his mission a little difficult at times. He has to convince us that of all the Utopias on offer, his is the best and the most likely to come into being, if only we would all rise up and make it happen. Unfortunately for him, most of us are just too busy dealing with the mundane practicalities of daily life to follow him into the sun and beyond.

Preacher is not a new addition to the male faces. There have always been men like him – visionaries, zealots, evangelists. Down the centuries, and in most countries, we've seen Preachers emerge to make their stand for a better world. He's been, among other things, a Puritan, a Maoist, a Marxist, a Chartist, a Nazi. In this millennium, he could well be on the extreme left or on the extreme right of the political spectrum. Wherever he is, it's never, ever, in the middle. Alternatively, he could be a religious devotee, but one of the more fundamentalist and disturbing kind – not, for example, a Buddhist. Preachers are especially vocal in parts of Europe, middle America and the Middle East. In England, you'll find him among anti-hunt protesters, or lying prostrate in front of earthmovers attempting to carve a new motorway through the countryside. Preacher especially relishes anti-globalisation marches in genteel, historic European cities. He has never relinquished his membership of the Socialist Workers Party, even though its activities have long since been ignored by MI5. Whatever his cause, Preacher fervently believes in its worth and will do whatever is necessary to promote it to the rest of us, for, in his mind, he is committed to a new and better world, just so long as it mirrors his own moral and political compass.

Can Preacher be trusted in love?

Research in America reveals that while religious people may disapprove of affairs more strongly than others, they end up being as unfaithful as the rest of us. To put it another way, unless his cause is free love and sexual experimentation, you shouldn't find him any less trustworthy than most other faces. Some Preachers do find that all that performing on the soapbox makes them feel ever so randy, in which case they have no choice but to go off and satisfy the most basic of adult needs. If your Preacher seems like he's one of these men, you may have to rein him in. Alternatively, just throw cold water over him when he finally steps off the podium.

Is Preacher romantic?

If romance is what you are after, forget this guy. Whatever religious or political ideology he espouses, it's unlikely to include a manifesto for bringing his loved one chocolates and flowers, whispering sweet nothings in her ear, or whisking her off to exotic foreign parts. This warns you about one of Preacher's most common characteristics – he is into frugality, self-sacrifice, devotion to duty and sparseness. He is not necessarily a bundle of laughs. His intense manner should warn you of his serious and parsimonious approach to life. Preacher has very buttoned-down emotions, which is interesting given his highly emotional performance at the pulpit. So if you want a swinging night with him, get him to lecture you first and then, when he's all in a sweat and excited, head for the bedroom.

Is Preacher the marrying kind?

Again, this depends on his particular stance. If he's an evangelist, it's more than likely he'll believe in the state of marriage – most religions do. Most religions also believe in traditional male roles – man as head of the family, with wife, kids and the rest following dutifully behind. If he's on the political left, his views on marriage could be much more liberal, in which case you'll have a harder job getting him to say 'I do'.

What sort of woman does Preacher go for?

No question about this, she'll have to be in the party just like him, and she'll have to complement his political image, not detract from it. However, this man is not so singularly minded about sex as to shy away from a little experimentation, at least when he's younger and at university. If he's at this stage in his life, he may be tempted by someone who knows nothing about politics or religion and cares even less. Beneath his earnest and staid exterior, Preacher may well fantasise about the mini-skirted girl down at the supermarket, or the young teacher at his kids' school. Of course, he'd be too shy, and scared, to do anything about it, but he might, if he's really brave, invite her to the next rally.

Occasionally, Preachers have been known to go for the very opposite of themselves – a woman who is a tigress in bed, sexually switched on, and up for a laugh. Such arrangements tend not to last long. He enjoys it, but she gets bored. For the most part, you can expect Preacher to settle down with a woman who agrees with almost everything he says, toes the party line and enjoys the occasional political meeting just as much as he does. Preacher and his partner will read the same newspapers, watch the same TV programmes, go to the same political rallies, agree about which politicians and religious leaders deserve to be shot, and where to go for their two-week annual holiday.

What is Preacher like as a father?

He'd hate to admit it but he's not very good father material. He's too narrow minded and too busy. When his kids are young he's either pre-occupied with the next manifesto or he's off to London for the big demonstration. When his children are babies they won't be able to object to being hauled along for the march, but when they get big enough to say 'no chance' things can get fraught for this male face. Many children of Preachers rebel against their fathers' strident views to the extent that they end up taking the very opposite route, believing in nothing except having a good time or, worse, becoming Corporate Men or Cool Posers. To be sure, Preacher is a devoted father, but not so much towards his family as towards his followers or his congregation.

Could you work for Preacher?

Don't work for him unless you believe in his particular mantra. He's not a man who is accommodating of alternative viewpoints, so you'd have to keep your counsel when he got on his soapbox at staff meetings. Also, you may well find this male face to be quite dictatorial and authoritarian when he's got a toehold in the organisation. Suddenly to find he actually has some power, albeit just as a senior manager, can really turn him on.

Would you like Preacher as a friend?

Preacher doesn't have friends. He has political acquaintances. If you are one of these, you'll probably get on okay, but be aware that this political animal has quite well-developed Machiavellian tendencies. If he's on the up and up, or even on the down, watch your back. He may appear quiet, dull and uninteresting, devoted only to the party, but there is often more going on behind the scenes with this male face than he gives away. So look out for those Preachers who seem just a little too politically ambitious. Remember, politics is not for the squeamish.

Scientifically speaking

Neo-Marxist theory, of the type espoused for example by Antonio Gramsci, argues that political and religious dogma is a form of ideology that attempts to subsume alternative, freer ways of thinking and acting under its sway. Some Marxists, such as Louis Althusser, go further and suggest that those of us who see through this process are enlightened while the rest are benighted 'cultural dopes'. This may be a rather limited perspective, but it does explain how Preacher can fervently believe in something that he cannot see and doesn't exist, yet for him appears tantalisingly real.

Is Preacher the man for you?

There is rarely a neutral opinion over this guy. You either support him or you don't. His uncompromising views and beliefs don't make him an easy man to like, but for those who relish the cut and thrust of heated political debate he may well make the perfect partner. If you can tolerate his puritanical tendencies and his habit of slipping into lecturing mode at the drop of a hat, maybe give him a try. At least you'll learn something about politics.

To sum up

Unless you are a budding Preacher yourself, or just enjoy an argument, never get into a political or religious debate with this male face. You cannot win and you cannot change his mind. Preacher is a fanatic. He sees his life as a quest to change society big-time. He's on a mission. Are you on the same mission? Unless you are, and totally committed to his cause, forget it. This man does not compromise. He does not shift his views. No matter what his intellect might tell him, his heart is not for turning. Best make sure yours isn't either.

HOW TO SPOT A PREACHER

Look out for him at Speaker's Corner in Hyde Park, London. He'll be very visible – he won't be sitting on a fence.

HOW DOES PREACHER PERFORM IN THE BEDROOM?

This guy is better on the platform than under the duvet.

WHAT IF PREACHER IS YOUR PARTNER?

Mr and Mrs Preacher. It's the only route to happiness – and a quiet life.

MOST LIKELY TO SAY

'You know I'm right.'

KEY QUESTION

Surely Utopia can only ever be a figment of our individual imaginings and yearnings?
Answer: Yes, that is true, but don't tell Preacher.

RISKER

Main characteristics

Always optimistic; bruised, bloodied but unbowed; overdrawn at the bank; likes to push his luck; someone who never doubts he will win.

What's he like?

Life is a rollercoaster and most of us take a tumble now and again. That's okay, life should never be boring. But what of those men whose very being is driven by risk, adventure and gambles? What do we make of those who appear to have it all but then, for no apparent logical reason, put it all at risk? For these men life is not just a rollercoaster – it's free-form rock climbing in the Grand Canyon. Such men are the Riskers of the species – they risk everything, habitually, constantly, without hesitation. Their wins may be colossal, their losses breathtaking, but either way their fingers are never far from the self-destruct button.

Riskers get their buzz from gambling for the highest stakes, living on the edge – literally and metaphorically. Risker likes to gamble everything, issuing the greatest challenge to fate – that way he gets the greatest surge of adrenaline. It may be poker, horse racing, relationships, white-water rafting, competitive rock climbing, camel trekking through the Gobi desert. Whether it is risking his money, his job, his marriage or his life, Risker keeps coming back for more, time and again. The risk taking is a drug and there is no known antidote.

His addiction to risk is the only thing that is predictable about Risker. Just when you think you've got him sussed, off he goes again. He can never settle. He rarely relaxes. He gets his kicks from bouncing back from adversity, in which he constantly finds himself. This tells us something about Risker – he cannot abide a quiet, comfortable life, although he does appreciate the routine and security of family life for a month or so. He gets switched on only when his back is to the wall, when the chips are down, when he's hanging by his fingertips. This incredible male face is truly happy only when he is living at the extreme margins of life, laughing at fate. There are many men out there like him.

Can Risker be trusted in love?

Just so long as Risker is not addicted to dangerous sex with multiple partners, you should be safe with him in terms of love. Most Riskers are men who prefer to risk money and life rather than relationships. But if your Risker is into the darker side of human sexuality, tread very carefully indeed. The danger is you may not be aware of this aspect of his character until it is too late. You and he could be married with kids when, out of the blue, something happens and you are faced with the awful realisation that your loved one has a hidden sexual side. He could have been cruising for gay sex on Hampstead Heath and been picked up by the police. He could be addicted to unprotected sex with working girls, or he could have been collecting stuff off the Internet that no decent person would wish to see. Of course, none of these activities prove he doesn't love you, but they do indicate he's willing to risk his relationship with you in order to continue doing them.

Is Risker romantic?

Romance can work in two ways – with the big expensive gesture, and the small inexpensive thoughtful one. Ideally, it should be a surprise either way – the unexpected always has the best result in love. With Risker, you can get both the big one and the little one. He is often quite good at understanding human nature – he's had a first-rate education trying to understand himself – so he'll likely know which you prefer. However, if Risker does suddenly come over romantic, it could be a sign that he's about to pack his bags for the Himalayas, that he's just won on the horses, or that he's building up to say sorry about a gamble that didn't quite pay off.

Is Risker the marrying kind?

So long as illicit sex is not his buzz, marriage and Risker can work out fine. Very few Riskers remain single for long. They appreciate the security and stability that comes from having a loving partner at home. But let's be frank, Riskers are not the best bet for an unstressful partnership. Their compulsion to jeopardise life, limb or bank balance is inevitably going to get in the way of the relationship at some point. Your Risker could be an excellent sportsman but one who undermines his reputation or health through gambling or drugs. It may be that your Risker is a very successful businessman, someone who has constantly gambled and found it's paid off handsomely for him. Such men often find they get bored when their mini-empires are running smoothly and their bank balance is in the millions. They feel the urge to go for the next big project, the next big risk, only this time they risk everything they've worked for. This may seem strange to ordinary folk. Most of us would just sell up and head for the Caribbean. But money is not what drives Riskers – it's the gamble with fate. They are pitting themselves against the odds. Often they will come out of it okay if not better off, at least financially. In fact, some Riskers are very wealthy men. But there are other Riskers who are constantly in debt. It then becomes a question of balance and judgement – his balance of mind, and your judgement about whether he's the man for you.

What sort of woman does Risker go for?

This male face is shrewd enough to look for women who won't give him too hard a time over his addiction to risk. He may go for a woman like himself, another adventurer seeking to sail the Atlantic single-handed or hang-glide off Everest. Those Riskers who are into sex escapades will likely choose a woman who is their very opposite as there is no better way to conceal such behaviour from prying eyes than by having a dutiful and respectable wife at home. Ultimately, whether Risker's addiction involves casinos, business deals, shark-diving or sex, he'll need someone alongside him who is at the very least prepared to understand what makes him tick. She'll have to be patient and understanding and yet also able to let him know very clearly where the line is that he mustn't cross. Importantly, she must be stronger than him, and he must know it.

What is Risker like as a father?

Becoming a father can be just the catalyst Risker needs in order to begin working to change his behaviour, thereby developing into another male face. For the first time in his life, he has someone who needs him and, importantly, relies on him. If you are his partner and you thought that role was yours, think again. He may love you but that in itself won't be enough to curb his addiction. A child might make the difference. Suddenly, the idea of putting his life or the family home at risk seems even more bizarre than it did before. Now there is a son or daughter who, in his or her innocence, expects dad to be there come what may. Risker may tone down his behaviour – or he may not. He may simply carry on as he's always done, oblivious to the damage and stress it causes his family. Having his child is a risk in itself. However, as the child's mother, at least this is one risk you have some control over.

Could you work for Risker?

Unlike most male faces, Risker is not the sort to be holding down a steady job in industry or commerce. If you do find him there, it's likely to be a temporary respite from his more extreme pastimes. If he's your boss, I wouldn't be too concerned – unless he's about to gamble the company profits.

Would you like Risker as a friend?

Why not? He is an interesting character and he's going to have some fascinating stories to tell, just so long as he gets back from his travels and adventures in one piece. Don't expect him to tell all down at the Golden Lion, unless he's had several first, but nevertheless if he's a friend, you'll end up watching him succumb to his addiction with either horror or fascination – most likely a little of both.

Scientifically speaking

As British sociologist Anthony Giddens argues, we live in an age of heightened risk because we are increasingly forced to place our fate in the hands of anonymous external agents and agencies. We have to trust the plane won't fall out of the sky, but there's a risk it might. Risk, and its consequences, threatens to disrupt our security and our lives. So why does Risker take the chance? He does it because, perversely, he wants to control his fate. Every time he puts his future on the line he's directly challenging fate, taking control of his destiny, experimenting with trust and coming out ahead. Risker may not be able to do anything about a meteor falling on his head, but through his planning and preparation he can certainly minimise the odds against falling off the Matterhorn.

Is Risker the man for you?

This is one to avoid if you want an easy life. Don't take this guy on as a long-term project unless you've realised what drives him. He may seem quite ordinary to you but beneath the apparently smooth surface he's anything but. The key to Risker is knowing what his addiction is, as some are easier to handle and tolerate than others. Also, you must accept that whatever it is that gives him his buzz, it's not you. He may love you and never want to lose you, he may treat you like his queen, but none of this will stop him repeating what can be damaging behaviour. Don't imagine he's doing this to punish you, even though it may well feel like that on occasions. He's simply caught in a trap of compulsive behaviour, and he's going to carry on like this whether you are with him or not.

If you've come to realise that you're involved with a Risker, there is a very important judgement you must make about him. Given that he's not going to change, what are his chances of success at whatever gamble he takes? Is he a clever, astute Risker, someone who knows the odds and plays them out with care? Does he prepare himself diligently before taking off for a trek through the Amazon rainforest, or is he one of those men who gets in a rowing boat and just heads south from Portsmouth one day? Many Riskers are excellent gamblers. They play the game to win, seek to minimise the odds against them and come out ahead more often than not, although they will certainly lose occasionally. In other words, is your Risker a winner or a loser? Find out before you hang over the precipice with him holding the rope.

To sum up

Life is a challenge for all of us, but Risker has turned it into an art form. Whatever it is that turns him on, make sure it turns you on too, or you will forever be that comfort zone at home to which he returns when he's spent his energy on his latest risk fix. He will always come home, even though it's only ever as a temporary respite before his next adventure. You are his rock, his roots, the shoulder on which to lay his weary head. You'll get so annoyed and angry at his latest escapade or predicament, you will fear for his life in the Himalayas, you will fear for your financial security during Ascot week, but he will never leave you. That is one risk he wouldn't undertake.

HOW TO SPOT A RISKER

He'll either be at the casino, heading for the Sahara desert, or off to see some venture capitalists.

HOW DOES RISKER
PERFORM IN THE BEDROOM?

He has cyclical periods of sexual activity, seething with testosterone when he's in gambling mode, pretty dormant the rest of the time.

WHAT IF RISKER IS YOUR PARTNER?

Make sure you have separate bank accounts, have him well covered with life insurance and get him to have his fortune told.

MOST LIKELY TO SAY

'You always bring me luck – you are my lucky charm.'

KEY QUESTION

He thrives on it all, but what about you? Can you stand the pace?

Answer: Only if you are very resilient, very patient and don't lend him money.

ROMANCER

Main characteristics

Calculating seducer; a toxic lover; dislikes women but pursues them; likes to get in women's heads – and other parts; the proverbial wolf in sheep's clothing.

What's he like?

Every heterosexual man, at some time in his life, fancies himself as a bit of a lad, a womaniser, a Don Juan, but most men never act out this role. They live it in their heads, not in real life – it remains fantasy land for them. Those men who might be inclined to 'play the field' are either too scared or too insecure around women to become serial shaggers. However, there is one type out there who has perfected this role to such a degree that his whole life and being is structured to ensure he lives it out to the fullest extent. This man is Romancer. He is the arch sexual predator, artful, devious, seductive – a sexual animal who has learnt all the right moves in the game of love and romance.

Despite his relentless pursuit of sex, Romancer is not a true Don Juan or Casanova. Unlike these legendary lovers, Romancer doesn't really like women. What he's searching for is the feeling of power over them. Sure, he wants to have lots of women in his life, but not for companionship or friendship. For Romancer, women are merely the means to an end and that end is his own self-glory and confirmation of himself as a man. For him, seduction is less about sexual satisfaction than about sexual pursuit. The means are more important, and more exciting, than the end.

Can Romancer be trusted in love?

Can you trust the snake in the undergrowth? Hardly. But you can trust Romancer to act in a very predictable way. You can trust him always to have one eye on other women.

Although Romancer is fairly predictable in his actions and motivations, don't expect to read him like a book. He won't let his face slip, no matter how intimate you and he become. He is most unlikely ever to reveal his true feelings and agendas. However, Romancer does have a good knowledge of how intimacy works, at least in a quasi-emotional way. He uses this knowledge to gain access to women, break down their barriers and win their trust. He may well be married and in a relationship, but he will go from woman to woman with remarkable ease, usually having several in his life at one time. He is psychologically unable to be faithful, but he will always promise to be.

It's important not to confuse Romancer with other male faces. Many other men have affairs, too. In fact, the 2003 UK Survey of Sexual Attitudes reveals that one in ten men admits to adultery in the past five years; 55 per cent of both sexes admit to an affair at some point in their lives; and 6 per cent of husbands had sex with someone other than their wives in the past year. But only Romancer invests his sense of masculine identity in the sexual conquest of women.

Is Romancer romantic?

This male face needs no lessons in romance, but it doesn't come from the heart. Its origins are in the head, closely followed by the groin. His is a contrived, strategic intimacy, where love and passion conceal an agenda of pursuit and conquest.

Romancer is one of the most adept of all men at seducing women, courting them, instilling trust in them, and making them feel uniquely special and desirable. This is what he does. It is his reason for being. Everything else that goes on in Romancer's life is merely the background setting to his central aim, which is to capture women's hearts. If he can't get through to the heart, he'll settle for the body.

I interviewed several women who had had experiences with Romancer. All told the same story. Here was a man who understood them, who listened to them, who treated them as equals but who demonstrated a compelling masculine passion. His romantic moves were expertly played out and followed a pattern. He tended to move in slowly at first, never signalling his intentions and never acting clumsily. Unless it was a spontaneous encounter, Romancer usually got to know his victim well before he made a move. The hook he dangled would invariably be mutuality and empathy, not sex.

Mutuality and empathy are absolutely key to Romancer's technique. His strategy is to give the impression that he and you are on the same wavelength, that you share the same interests, and, most importantly, that you speak the same emotional language. Romancer is particularly tuned in to those women who are lonely or feel isolated. They could be in relationships that have outlived their usefulness, or they may be emotionally distressed and carrying baggage from past relationships. Both types of women have something in common – they are vulnerable. His strategy is to use that vulnerability against them by giving the impression that he is a man who understands their situation and their emotional pain. Having established this level of empathy and mutuality, and of course trust, Romancer turns up the heat of intimacy until he calculates the moment is right for making his final move.

Each of the women I interviewed fell for their Romancer in a big way. Several were already married when they got involved with him. Others were looking for love and thought they had found it with him. They eventually discovered how wrong they were. Ironically, as the painful realisation dawned that he was not the man he appeared to be, so some of the women felt compelled to pursue him more relentlessly, sometimes debasing themselves sexually in the process.

So long as Romancer plays it carefully and is consistent in his moves, few women can resist him. Long before he has bedded them, most will have started to fall in love a little. He understands that women want to be loved by a man who appreciates them, values them as individuals, desires them as sexual beings, respects their individuality, and understands something of their history. His skill is in appearing to offer all this and more.

Is Romancer the marrying kind?

This male face may well be married and, to all appearances, quite happily so. Indeed, he is likely to be quite contented as a married man. After all, as he sees it, he has everything – a loving and faithful wife at home, and numerous other women coming in and out of his life on a regular basis. For him, this is bliss. Of course, such situations only last for as long as he doesn't get found out. If this happens, he may find himself single once more, in which case he becomes what one self-confessed American Romancer describes as 'the toxic bachelor'.

What sort of woman does Romancer go for?

For Romancer, there is the marrying kind and the shagging kind. In order to decide which category is appropriate for you, he will have to assess to what degree he can manipulate you. The more amenable you are to being manipulated or tolerant of his behaviour, the more likely he'll want a long-term relationship with you. He knows that many wives reconcile themselves to their husbands' infidelities, seeing it as part of their characters and therefore unable to be changed. He is also aware that so long as he doesn't admit to any emotional involvement with those women he seduces, his wife is more likely to forgive, if not exactly forget. Many women consider emotional infidelity to be far more dangerous and damaging to them than physical unfaithfulness. In the UK, over two-thirds of couples now stay together after one or other partner has had an affair. These are some of the considerations Romancer takes into account when he assesses your long-term status in his life.

What is Romancer like as a father?

Like Chameleman and many other male faces, Romancer does compartmentalisation very well. For him, his kids may well be sacrosanct, but that won't stop him making a play for his teenaged daughter's girlfriends, or the mothers he meets when collecting his kids from school.

Could you work for Romancer?

If you are his PA, inevitably you will become embroiled in his complicated life. You will have to lie for him to his boss and to his wife, covering his tracks when he should be at home or at a business meeting but is, instead, parked somewhere in a country lane with his latest conquest. If you are male, he'll seem like any other bloke, a bit of a lad but otherwise normal. If you are a woman employee, within seconds of meeting you he will have assessed your sexual potential. After that, you can only wait, watch and wonder. He may never make any move at all, or he could be planning one.

Would you like Romancer as a friend?

Romancer is something of a loner, unlikely to be seen in those all-male groups that attract Uniform Man and Club Man. This is partly because Romancer is altogether too intelligent to want to be associated with such a macho group of men – they'd cramp his style.

Scientifically speaking

For American pro-feminist writer Michael Messner, the sexual objectification of women by men is largely a 'rhetorical performance' that rarely gets acted out as real-life dominance. Similarly, according to American sociologist Donald Sabo, many men end up suffering a kind of 'sexual schizophrenia', their minds leading them towards serial shagging, their hearts towards emotional intimacy. What is different about Romancer is that he is one of those few men who is prepared to sacrifice an intimate, emotional relationship with a woman in return for a self-destructive and impoverished display of love and affection. So while Romancer may appear to be in the pursuit of intimacy, he is actually in retreat from it.

Is Romancer the man for you?

Despite his poisonous character, there may be times in your life when you'd relish having the attention of a man like

Romancer. He'd make you feel good, he'd be as romantic as you wanted him to be, and he'd pursue you relentlessly. For a while at least, you'd feel on top of the world. If you are in a marriage that has long lost its sparkle, and as a result you feel you've lost your feminine allure, Romancer is the man to restore it. If you are unattached and a little lonely at times, you can be sure that Romancer will come knocking on your door, or texting you, at precisely those moments when you'd most welcome his attention.

But always remember, if you play with this man you are playing with fire. As time goes by, the suspicion that your lover is not all he seems will sneak up on you. You will come to doubt whether he actually was at a business meeting the evening he couldn't phone you, or whether his last-minute trip to Paris really was so last minute after all. Don't take this man on as a project for change. If you do get involved, do so with your eyes open. Use him as he uses you.

To sum up

Most men can be cads at some time in their lives, many flirt with infidelity and all fantasise about the seduction techniques that might best work with a particular fancy of theirs. However, only Romancer makes a career out of this.

As Romancer stalks his prey, he moves with ease through the undergrowth, appearing in the office or supermarket, in the committee room, or at the private fitness centre. Women, young and not so young, are his target. Don't think that you can spot him by his dress or his looks. You cannot. In that respect he is very like Chameleman, but with one important difference. Romancer has one aim in life and that is to expand his list of bedded women. His real pulling power for women is his capacity to think like them, to predict their actions and responses, and to appear so genuine when he is on the pull. He knows women very well indeed. They are not, for him, some mysterious species, but a very clear and transparent one. However, to condemn Romancer for being unreliable or untrustworthy is pointless. It is like condemning the tiger for prowling the jungle.

HOW TO SPOT A ROMANCER

You won't, at least not at first. Start being suspicious of any man who seems to know how you tick but isn't so forthcoming about his past relationships.

HOW DOES ROMANCER PERFORM IN THE BEDROOM?

Knows all the moves and should play them out with a degree of skill and accomplishment, though you may well find there's a certain mechanistic style to his love-making – more planned than passionate.

WHAT IF ROMANCER IS YOUR PARTNER?

Did you sense it before you read this book? Probably. But did you dare admit it to yourself? Less likely.

MOST LIKELY TO SAY

'I love you.'

KEY QUESTION

Should you play with Romancer, given he is such an emotional risk?

Answer: Yes, but only if you do so for the moment, not for life. Best play him at his own game – he hates being used.

ROTTWEILER

Main characteristics

Lager drinker; wears Union Jack shorts; loves his mates; national flag hanging outside his bedroom window; opinionated but uneducated.

What's he like?

In an age when men are increasingly expected to 'get in touch with their inner selves', there remains a large percentage of male faces who are stereotypically masculine. These guys could no more get in touch with their feminine 'essence' than they could give up overtaking on the inside. Their personalities have 'unreconstituted male' stamped all over them. We've all come across this type of guy, the man who, for example, once he's behind the wheel of a vehicle, seems compelled to prove that he's the fastest, quickest driver around, regardless of the cost to others. But you'd be wary of challenging him about his lack of courtesy on the road because this is one man you sense it would be best to avoid in an argument. Blessed, or cursed, with an over-load of testosterone this guy is Rottweiler. Some refer to him as 'white van man', not only because it often seems he's driving this type of vehicle but because he's doing so in such a way as to intimidate every other road user.

The Rottweiler is a large, black, scary breed of a dog, not the sort of animal to pet and pamper. Its human namesake is just the same. Physically strong, but no intellectual, Rottweiler's raw masculinity can manifest itself anywhere, but particularly at sporting events. Across Europe, Rottweiler is known for his passionate love of football. Some of his type also like the occasional weekend political rally.

The UK version of this male face loves his home town best, but when he has to travel, quiet, sophisticated European cities are his preferred destination, or perhaps the neon lights of Benidorm. The dignified Burgers of Brussels and Bruges can only look on with incredulity and dismay when Rottweiler pays a visit, although the French CRS (riot police) have been known to welcome his appearance in Paris. Dressed up, he can be seen in short black leather jacket, white T-shirt and jeans, while in warmer climes he favours Union Jack shorts over which hangs his extended beer gut. His manner and appearance suggest a man totally lacking any self-regard, which is true, especially when his prejudices have been fuelled by alcohol. He has a lot of pride in those things that give meaning to his life – football team, national identity, his family, his mates.

Can Rottweiler be trusted in love?

Strangely enough, yes. Despite, or more likely because of, his very macho behaviour, Rottweiler prefers male to female company. In common with Uniform Man and Club Man, Rottweiler is happiest when he's with his mates. So other than the occasional fling after getting his juices fired up late one night at a lap-dancing club, Rottweiler is one of your more trustworthy men.

Is Rottweiler romantic?

If you listened in to his talk when he's down at the pub with his mates, you'd imagine that Rottweiler is a real ladies' man, a killer lover, a serial seducer. He's only this in his head. He has no chance of being Romancer or Backpacker. He hasn't the aptitude, the skill, the patience, the intelligence or the inclination. It's the same with romance. Like Neanderthal, he doesn't really understand women, certainly not modern ones. Rottweiler is the sort of guy who will pick up a bunch of flowers for his girlfriend at the same time as he fills his car with petrol – a last-minute impulse purchase if he feels it'll pay dividends later that night.

Is Rottweiler the marrying kind?

Marriage is something most Rottweilers end up stumbling into, almost by accident. They'll stay with mum until they're kicked out or their bedroom has started to resemble a disaster zone, and then they'll look for a mum replacement. This is likely to be some local girl who has her own reasons for being with this guy. Either she'll be thinking it's time to have a family and Rottweiler is available to perform the necessary role, or she'll be in love with him. Whether he's in love with her matters a little less. Sure, he'll say he is, but she's a bit weary, and a bit wary, of always having to ask first.

What sort of woman does Rottweiler go for?

Most Rottweilers don't do the choosing in love. They may think they do but the fact is they get chosen. His woman may make it look like he's made the first move, but he hasn't, she has. This has the effect of convincing Rottweiler of his expertise as a seducer, which is a necessary illusion if he's to be a half-decent lover in bed. If he realised that he'd been the one selected and thereby shrewdly manipulated into the relationship, it would certainly dampen his ardour. How it works is that Rottweiler's sense of masculinity is one of the most fragile of all the male faces. However, the insubstantiality of his maleness is something he cannot be confronted with. If his masculinity is threatened, that is when you see the animal in him rear its head. Rottweiler adopts stereotypical male postures simply because he thinks this is how 'real men' behave. The fact that he surrounds himself with other Rottweilers serves to reinforce this misconception. Rottweiler doesn't have the necessary reasoning skills and emotional insight to understand what makes him tick. What he does have is his infamously short temper. This, coupled with his brittle masculine self-esteem, makes for an explosive mix.

What is Rottweiler like as a father?

Rottweiler is likely to dote on his offspring – just keep him on a lead when he pushes the pram. This is the man to protect his kids from junior wannabe Rottweilers during schooldays, but ask him to assess the quality of his kid's BA dissertation and you're in trouble. You need Libman for that. Rottweiler may have left school at an early age, but he'll be the first to 'sort out the headmaster' should he have the effrontery to expel his little Jason for threatening a teacher. On the plus side, Rottweiler will always get Jason a ticket for the local cup match, and he'll be proud to stand there in the Kop alongside him. Just make sure you prime Jason to get him home safely afterwards.

Could you work for Rottweiler?

Most Rottweilers have neither the qualifications nor the aptitude for succeeding in organisational life, so they're unlikely to make it to director level. However, a small number do end up running their own businesses and can even become very wealthy as a result. Most towns and cities will have Rottweiler-run firms, and not all will be of a dubious nature. Some will be very respectable. If he's your boss, he shouldn't be unduly difficult to work for, but neither his Porsche nor his Armani suit will hide the fact that here is a male face with basic animal instincts.

Would you like Rottweiler as a friend?

Only if you are a Rottweiler yourself, in which case you and the gang will feel very safe together out on the town at weekends. Occasionally, you and he will find yourself in the back of a police van, bruised and bleeding, but isn't that what lads are supposed to get up to on a Friday night?

Scientifically speaking

As American sociologist Michael Kaufman argues, aggression – a vying for predominance – is one of the fundamental dynamics of masculinity. In many societies and many types of male-dominated organisations, being aggressive is seen as natural masculine behaviour – not only acceptable, but expected. Not being aggressive in such situations may even be dangerous – think of the football team or the armed forces. If they are seen as weak and ineffectual, males can be bullied and abused. What Rottweiler is doing is acting out this limited expression of masculinity. He can control it if he wishes, it's just that he chooses not to, or more accurately, he's never learnt how to.

Is Rottweiler the man for you?

There are a lot of Rottweilers around. Unfortunately, they are quite a common male face. They are a bit like Neanderthal, a left-over from a more primitive age of man, but that won't stop them from continuing to surface for some time to come. Unlike Neanderthal, Rottweiler doesn't dislike women; he just doesn't understand them too well. Again unlike Neanderthal, Rottweiler does attract certain women, usually those who welcome his rugged, unapologetic masculinity. They feel safe with him, walking into a crowded bar. His paternalistic manner complements their sense of femininity, and, most important, they can manage him. If Rottweiler's male characteristics are the sort to turn you on, go for it. He's a very distinct, but simple, male face. There is none of the complicated depth that comes with types such as Sigmund, and he'll be much more faithful than either Manchild or Chameleman.

However, if you prefer someone who reads *The Times* rather than the *Sun*, Rottweiler would quickly bore you. Don't live with him unless you too enjoy the simpler things of life – lager, pub food, Saturday night television, and holidays in Torremolinos.

To sum up

Rottweiler is a fairly standard type of male, not especially complex and not particularly unusual. He has his good points and his bad ones. He can be very loyal and a good companion to have in a tight spot. His view of women is very traditional – that is, he tends to see them as confused, contradictory and irrational creatures who need a bloke around, which shows he doesn't understand them at all. Despite the problems this ignorance may cause his partner, Rottweiler can be a loving and faithful husband, a reliable soulmate, so long as you create the impression he's in control.

HOW TO SPOT A ROTTWEILER

He's usually with his mates, at the head of the gang, leading the chanting, the aggressive gesturing and the drinking.

HOW DOES ROTTWEILER PERFORM IN THE BEDROOM?

Given that a lot of older Rottweilers are overweight, this type can be surprisingly energetic lovers – no good at the end of an evening's drinking, but can rise to the occasion on a Sunday morning. Needs pampering afterwards.

WHAT IF ROTTWEILER IS YOUR PARTNER?

Well, you chose him and you probably knew exactly what you were getting into.

MOST LIKELY TO SAY

'Hey you, what are you looking at?!'

KEY QUESTION

You are expecting his baby, but do you take him along to the ante-natal classes or not?

Answer: Yes. As with all men, being a father is something he can only learn through experience.

SIGMUND

Main characteristics

Lots of inner angst; Oedipus complex; troubled self-esteem; loving, caring, reliable and trustworthy; desires to be a good father and husband.

What's he like?

Sigmund Freud was the founding father of psychoanalysis. Through his writings he left behind a wealth of knowledge and theory about the human condition and our inner selves. Much of his work centred around men's unresolved inner conflict with their parents, either mother or father. He argued that much of our lives are spent in an endless quest for one or other parent's approval, something that can remain tantalisingly elusive to us, depending on our relationship with those who brought us into the world. Freud described this phenomenon as the Oedipus complex, which went on to become the cornerstone of classical psychoanalysis. Simply put, Freud argued that fathers, as the possessor of the penis, inspire a fear of castration in boys, mainly through their power as the family patriarch. Meanwhile, the mother, according to the rule of the father, becomes the forbidden object that her son must both desire and yet reject.

Freud acknowledged that while our parents remain power-fully influential on our subconscious motives and actions in life, most of us move on from constantly desiring their approval. We come to realise that our parents, important as they are to us, do not ultimately define us as adults. Only we can do that for our-selves. But there are some men who never quite manage to achieve this peaceful state of mind. Instead, they go through life constantly feeling the need for parental approval and valida-tion. Such a man is Sigmund.

As most psychoanalysts will tell you, there are surprising numbers of men out there who are attempting to manage, on a regular basis, their ambiguous feelings for their mothers or fathers. There are few, if any, men who do not, at some point in their adult lives, look to their father for approval. Not many would admit to this, even if they recognised it, seeing it as some-how demeaning of them as men. Countless numbers of men take up careers or relationships simply because they believe that by doing so they will receive their parents' validation of them as sons. Yet despite this, millions of men never really feel close to either parent. They feel that their parents do not know them as adults, and do not understand them. They want to demonstrate their love for, and to, their parents, but find it a difficult, if not impossible, emotion to express.

Sigmund is typical of such men, but also different. He lives out this inner conflict in a very extreme way. Many Sigmunds are high achievers, leaders in their chosen field, high flyers in industry, academics, writers, highly qualified professionals, but a real feeling of being successful eludes them. They always feel less than they actually are.

Whether Sigmund's parents do it knowingly or not depends on the case, but they inevitably come to wield an unhealthy influence over their son. Some parents habitually withhold approval so as to remind Sigmund that he is still their child and thus under their influence and control. In most cases, it is one or other parent who is most dominant in Sigmund's life, not both. Which one it is depends on the unique circumstances and experiences of Sigmund's upbringing. Many of the unresolved anxieties about male power and potency are caught up in Sigmund's character and being.

Can Sigmund be trusted in love?

Most Sigmunds will attempt to manage their inner conflict by creating structures of stability and permanence in their lives, which are underpinned by trust. Sigmund is one of your more trustworthy male faces. He is troubled, unsure, unsettled and often ill at ease with himself, but he is astute enough to know that being serially unfaithful isn't going to help his situation. However, should your Sigmund be the son of a very wayward father or mother, different rules could apply. Some Sigmunds go on to repeat and replicate the behaviour of that parent who is most dominant and influential on their subconscious. It is not inevitable, but never forget, as poet Philip Larkin put it, 'They fuck you up your mum and dad, they may not mean to but they do.'

Is Sigmund romantic?

Once he's fallen in love with his soulmate, expect much from Sigmund in terms of romance. He is a man with deep feelings of love and passion, and he's very capable of demonstrating this through his romantic actions. Some Sigmunds love the written word. They write endless poems to their loved one – many historians have speculated that Shakespeare's confused and traumatic family background was a major motivation behind his drive to become the world's greatest wordsmith. Modern-day

Sigmunds are likely to be quite spontaneous in their demonstration of love and desire, presenting their loved one with all the traditional gifts a besotted man can bestow.

Is Sigmund the marrying kind?

As much if not more than any other face, Sigmund is the marrying kind. If marriage is not for either of you, be confident that this man can remain in a committed partnership with the same woman all his life. Divorce and separation would be most traumatic for him. Many male faces can move in and out of relationships with surprising alacrity, but not so Sigmund. He is one of those men who can suffer very badly if a relationship fails. Suddenly, as he sees it, he is experiencing disapproval and rejection from all those who have hitherto been the mainstays of his life.

What sort of woman does Sigmund go for?

Sigmund often finds a woman who is like his mother. Alternatively, he can choose someone who is the complete opposite, although this is less likely. Not surprisingly, as his wife, lover or partner, this situation is going to be very unsettling for you. You will find that your difficulties in the relationship are not with Sigmund so much as with his parents. However you play it, inevitably you will get entangled in the complex, sometimes volatile, relationship he has with them. Sigmund isn't consciously seeking a woman who will be acceptable to mum and dad, but that is what generally happens. The good news is that as time goes by and you become far more influential on Sigmund, so the influence of his parents will diminish. It will never entirely disappear, but he will come to see that you are a unique individual in your own right, not a mirror image of his mother.

What is Sigmund like as a father?

Given his taut emotional relationship with his dad, you'd expect Sigmund to be a difficult father in return but this is not necessarily the case. Sigmund can be an excellent dad, considerate and thoughtful, yet firm and consistent. He will be attempting to make amends for all the difficulties he had as a child, and he'll be desperate to ensure such relationship problems are not repeated. To what extent he may be successful in this is not easy to predict. Freud's theories apply to all individuals, not just to Sigmund, so to a greater or lesser degree we are all caught up in the Oedipus complex. There is no escape, but Sigmund does have a head start over the rest of us because he's been living at the sharp end of this theory all his life and therefore is likely to appreciate its consequences better than most.

Could you work for Sigmund?

Sigmund can be found in any sort of job or profession. He can be the manager or the shopfloor worker, the employer or the employee. A lot of Sigmunds work in male-dominated fields, such as sport and management. Whatever he is and wherever he is, you are likely to find him generally easy to get along with and not so bound up with his ego as many of the other male faces.

Would you like Sigmund as a friend?

You could do a lot worse. Sigmund is loyal to his friends and appreciative of their presence in his life. He's not really into the gregarious side of friendships, although some Sigmunds gravitate towards male bonding activities as a way of dealing with the unresolved masculinity complex handed down to them from their dads.

Scientifically speaking

It is notoriously difficult to apply any sort of objective scientific test to such concepts as Freud's Oedipus theory, so we are left with our own subjective judgements and intellectual analysis. There can be no doubt that fathers, whether hands-on or not, wield enormous subconscious influence over their children, especially their sons. Whether they do this wittingly or unwittingly is the issue. Sigmund is a product of a power tussle, and the handing down through the generations of many unresolved masculine issues. Sigmunds are not going to go away.

Is Sigmund the man for you?

This is one man you can take on in the hope, if not expectation, that through his love for you and yours for him, his life can improve. You should be very wary of going into any relationship with a man expecting to transform his sense of self, but with Sigmund there is the possibility of this happening. You shouldn't want him to become a Murdoch or a Gadgetman, or any face for that matter. You should be content with him as he is. What you might achieve with Sigmund is a resolving of his inner conflict with his parents, thereby enabling him to appreciate that he doesn't constantly have to fear his father's or his mother's disapproving gaze or harsh word. So long as he has your love and approval, and sensitivity to his situation, you and Sigmund can have a good life together.

Should you have your own unresolved issues with your parents, that too can be a powerful bond between Sigmund and yourself. At least there'll never be arguments about where to go for Christmas Day – you simply stay put in your own peaceful haven, free of both sets of in-laws.

To sum up

Sigmund is clearly a complex character, pulled as he is in several directions at once. Yet despite his difficulty in finding some inner peace within himself over his relationship, such as it was, with either his mother or his father, Sigmund does have many strengths. Firstly, he is usually a highly reflective person – he's had to learn to be during all those years of trying to manage unresolved feelings of love and hate towards his parents. Secondly, Sigmund can be a superb parent himself because he's determined never to impose feelings of rejection or negative judgement on his own children. This is a man who is capable of deep love and commitment. He makes a good husband or partner and he sees the family as the bedrock of his life. On top of all this, he is a very romantic and thoughtful guy. But remember his need for approval. Remember that much of what he does is undertaken with a gaze towards his parents, those omnipresent people in his life who stand and watch him from a distance. Learn about him, understand him, but don't patronise him or feel sorry for him, for he doesn't need it. What he does need is a partner who recognises his inner trauma and helps him appreciate that he is a man in his own right, and not forever his parents' child.

HOW TO SPOT A SIGMUND

Likely to be reading Freud. If not, make sure he gets a copy for Christmas.

HOW DOES SIGMUND PERFORM IN THE BEDROOM?

Okay, just so long as you never mention his dad at a critical moment.

WHAT IF SIGMUND IS YOUR PARTNER?

One of the best, but you'll have some trying times together. Then again, who doesn't?

MOST LIKELY TO SAY

'Has my mother rung yet?'

KEY QUESTION

You are getting married and are unsure where to have the ceremony. Should it be a simple do at the local registry office? An all-swinging do at the nearest four- or five-star hotel? A quiet and romantic ceremony in the Seychelles, with just the two of you and two witnesses?

Answer: The parents will want the second option, but you should go for the third – and you know why. You'll probably settle for the first.

TEDDY BEAR

Main characteristics

Reliable; sensitive; vulnerable; good listener; an easy man to like but unlikely to stir your loins.

What's he like?

One of the fascinating things about men is their variety. You think you've seen it all and then up pops a face that doesn't quite fit anywhere in the scheme of things, a man who doesn't seem quite as masculine as other males. Tempting as it might be to think that all men can be macho, assertive, overdosed with testosterone and predatory, you should know that there is one male face who has none of these characteristics. He is, in fact, very feminine. That doesn't make him gay, though there's no reason why he shouldn't be. It just makes him different from the Rottweilers, Murdochs and Alpha Males. Here is a guy who says yes to everyone, mostly because he can't find it in himself to say no. Say hello to Mr Nice Guy himself – Teddy Bear.

During my research I came across quite a number of these guys, and women who had them as friends or husbands. I named them Teddy Bears because they are cuddly, safe and gentle. They don't have a darker side. In fact, they don't have any side at all. They are just Teddy Bears. It seems to me that if every little girl has one, then every adult woman should have one too. These men are soft, comfortable, sensitive, always reliable and, in a very non-sexual way, quite attractive. They tend not to draw attention to themselves and they certainly lack the more assertive characteristics of the harder male faces. When a woman wants a male friend for dinner and nothing more, Teddy Bear is her man. He is totally trustworthy and very reflective. His feminine side has developed quite nicely over the years and whether gay or not, Teddy Bear always knows the right thing to say to his female friends, especially if they want a shoulder to cry on.

So what is the downside to what many women would see as the perfect man? The downside is he's not that shaggable. Women want to befriend him, not bestride him. They love his sensitive nature and gentle character, but he doesn't stir them inside. He may be lovely, but, for most women, he's just not naughty enough. This male face is much better as a friend than a lover. Women like him – how could they not? – but when it comes to sweaty passion they often prefer someone who is just a little rougher around the edges, someone a little dangerous. As one woman said to me, 'I love the Teddy Bear type of guys, but I get bored quickly. I end up wanting to fuck the bad boys instead.'

Can Teddy Bear be trusted in love?

Absolutely. If he's your friend, be sure that he will never rat on you when you reveal to him your secret passion for bondage, or your brief excursion into group sex during your last holiday in Jamaica. Teddy Bear will listen with wide eyes, but without moral judgement. If he's your husband, he may even countenance your desire to roam a little, take that hike across the

Andes or sample the exotic delights of Marrakesh, leaving him at home with the kids. He'll trust you and you can certainly trust him. Infidelity may be a word he understands, but the thought of practising it just wouldn't cross his mind.

Is Teddy Bear romantic?

If you think that men can only be romantic when they're on a promise, think again. Here is a man born for romance. Teddy Bear may live much of his life in a warm cocoon, rarely venturing into the cold and hostile outer world that surrounds him, but one of the things that gets him out there is love. Once Teddy Bear falls in love, he is totally absorbed and obsessed. He goes for it big-time. But he has to be very careful about which type of woman he falls for – like men, there are numerous faces of women and not all of them suit a Teddy Bear. One such woman I interviewed described how a Teddy Bear pursued her for several years. During this time, she saw other men, but, rather cruelly, she allowed Teddy Bear to continue his amorous moves simply because 'he became a sort of habit I liked to have around'. He would wine her, dine her, send her flowers and chocolates, even turning up unexpectedly with a box of carefully chosen cream cakes for her and her daughter. Little things and big things, romantic and loving, and done entirely from the heart. Yet she never slept with him. He was only rewarded with the occasional kiss. In fact, the more he pursued her, the worse she treated him.

Is Teddy Bear the marrying kind?

Many times I have asked women why they want to get married when it's easier to continue living with their partner. The usual reply is 'because I want my special day'. Rarely do you hear men say this. Teddy Bear is the exception to this male rule. He loves the wedding, the big do with family and friends. He'll be just as interested as you in the detail of it all – the flowers, the food, the ceremony, the honeymoon. What's more, you can go off and have a wild hen party safe in the knowledge that Teddy Bear will be home by midnight from his stag do.

When you return from your honeymoon, ready to embark on your life together, you will have a man who will follow his wedding vows to the letter. Teddy Bear is a guy who marries for life. He will not leave you. Alas, it is much more likely you will leave him.

What sort of woman does Teddy Bear go for?

Although he may be many a woman's dream man, at least up to a point, Teddy Bear is not good at recognising differences between women. This male face tends to see all women through an innocent lens – a sort of Virgin Mary syndrome. As you can imagine, this creates some problems for him. He trusts but without the emotional protection a more streetwise approach would afford him. He often finds himself attracted to Alpha Females, women who know they've got a househusband in the making, a man at home to support them while they go off and climb the corporate ladder. He too easily ends up with female versions of Backpacker and Romancer, women who love a little callously. Teddy Bear likes women as a species, and he's much less likely than other male faces to objectify them sexually. However, this one-dimensional view of women means he's very vulnerable to being used in love.

I've known Teddy Bears meet a woman and fall in love all in the space of a week. On Monday they have their first date together, a week later they are planning the wedding – or at least he is. She may like the idea but something starts to warn her off. When his 'soulmate' eventually pulls out, poor Teddy Bear is left beached, gasping for air, emotionally dying. What's worse, he often fails to understand what happened. He was reaching for the stars at precisely the moment she caught the next taxi.

The irony is that despite all his much admired qualities and emotional intelligence, Teddy Bear often ends up with the 'bad girls'. He gets messed about by girlfriends, and invariably gets hurt in a relationship. It's okay to be vulnerable but Teddy Bear does sometimes take it to extremes. Just why this should be is not always clear. Maybe his girlfriends can't resist taking advantage of him – dominating a man can initially be sexy but becomes rather tedious eventually. Maybe, despite his sensitive side, he doesn't really appreciate the difference between having a woman as a friend and having one as a lover. Many women discover they quickly fall in love with his sensitive side but find themselves constantly attracted to dangerous men, those likely to give them a hard time – in and out of bed.

What is Teddy Bear like as a father?

This is the sort of male face we'd all like as a dad – solid, dependable, loving, approachable and understanding. He'd be there on sports day, cheering you through the 800 metres. He'd buy you all the Harry Potter books, but be a little concerned that you might want to see *Lord of Rings*, given its age rating. He'd fork out for the series of horse-riding lessons, even though you quit in tears after twice falling off Blackie. And when you reached the very mature age of fifteen and introduced him to the love of your life, Andy, he would be there to pick you both up from the disco at precisely 11.00 p.m. If Teddy Bear was born to be a husband, he was equally born to be a father.

Could you work for Teddy Bear?

It's more likely that Teddy Bear would work for you. Some do make it to management positions, but it's mostly through chance rather than intent. Teddy Bear is not the most ambitious of male faces, and if you ever had to listen to him give a presentation at a group seminar you'd be forgiven for drifting off to sleep in the middle of it. Sure, he'd be full of innocent enthusiasm but his delivery would be much too monotonous to keep his audience awake. Don't expect to see this male face working in marketing or the city. He'd get slaughtered by the more ruthless male faces. The nearest he gets to high finance is working for a large bank – as a branch manager. He makes a good vicar, nurse, teacher, social worker, counsellor, secretary. He doesn't change careers much, and he prefers the relative security of the public sector to the cut and thrust of the private one. In the often harsh world of organisational politics, Teddy Bear is much too nice for his own good.

Would you like Teddy Bear as a friend?

Despite his feminine side, Teddy Bear finds it easier to have women as friends rather than lovers.

This is because most of his women friends realise it would spoil the friendship if they became lovers. Whether you are a man or a woman, you'll find few better friends than Teddy Bear. He'll always show delight when you phone, he'll always have time to listen to your account of your far more exciting life, and he'll leave you feeling so much better about yourself when you go. He won't judge or condemn, he won't betray. However, as his friend, you'll have to be prepared to experience the many ups and downs in his relationships, and when he's just lost the 'love of his life' he'll need you very much indeed. Just make sure you don't let him down.

Scientifically speaking

For feminist poststructuralists such as American writer Judith Butler, gender identity is a 'performative' process, developed by following socially acceptable male or female behaviour in everyday life. However, as Butler sees it, there is always the potential for subversion of these typical norms, and Teddy Bear is very much a disruptive male type, drawing as he does on dominant notions of femininity rather than those of masculinity. Ironically, Teddy Bear's subconscious resistance to powerful masculine tendencies turns out to be the most subversive aspect of his whole being.

Is Teddy Bear the man for you?

Before you decide, try to get some sense of what sort of woman you are. Remember, if you are attracted to dangerous men, Teddy Bear is not for you. You'll damage him. He may be emotionally intelligent, but his emotions are very exposed, not compartmentalised as they are with so many other male faces. In other words, are you good enough for him? If you want trust, honesty, love and companionship, Teddy Bear is your guy. If you want endless nights of rampant sex, and a little experimentation to spice it up, try Backpacker.

To sum up

Teddy Bear is not one of your more lively male faces and nor is he especially interesting. In fact, some would say he's a pretty boring type of guy, a man with a charisma deficit. Yet he's loyal and gentle, sensitive and trustworthy. Indeed, he's rather feminine, which is why he's often mistaken for being gay. Some Teddy Bears do have an ambiguous sexuality. He's the sort of guy who always tips the waiter, even if the waiter's insulted him, who apologises whenever someone steps on his foot, and who, despite the consequences, stays loyal to his barber. This is the one male face who is as innocent as he looks. Despite, or maybe because of, these traits, Teddy Bear is often let down by the women he loves. Some would say this is because he's naïve and falls in love too easily. His love life can be sad and lacking colour but Teddy Bear does have those qualities that many women love in a man – he will listen without judging, he will always return your call, he will never fail to turn up for a date, and he will stay away without complaint when you've got yourself tied up with Romancer or Risker.

HOW TO SPOT A TEDDY BEAR

Look for a man who seems invisible, who is easily missed, who never talks loudly, who doesn't attract attention to himself, who just seems very nice. Should be easy to spot.

HOW DOES TEDDY BEAR PERFORM IN THE BEDROOM?

Good at cuddles.

WHAT IF TEDDY BEAR IS YOUR PARTNER?

As you no doubt appreciate, you've got yourself a very steady bloke. Try to confine the dangerous men to fantasy land only.

MOST LIKELY TO SAY

'Go on, sit down and tell me all about it then.'

KEY QUESTION

You've a choice for a date – Cool Poser or Teddy Bear. Which one do you choose?
Answer: Both. Go to the best parties with Cool Poser and have a great time. Then go out with Teddy Bear and pour out your heart to him about what a bastard Cool Poser turned out to be.

TRAINSPOTTER

Main characteristics

Owns lots of brown cardigans and tweed jackets; always middle-aged; obsessively into data collection; loves twitching, fishing and the Great North Western railway.

What's he like?

Over the past twenty or so years, across the world, there has been a veritable explosion in the number of men taking up singular hobbies such as fishing, bird-watching, hiking and collecting. These men are not mere occasional hobbyists. They pursue their fixation avidly – for many, it has taken over their whole lives. It's as if a whole swathe of the male population has given up on the modern world and retreated to the comfort zone of habitual hobbying. Flying in to any major UK airport you'll see increasing numbers of men in anoraks standing, in all weathers, in a specially designated 'spotter zone', making notes on the planes as they take off and land. In many of the busier railway stations, you can see young and not so young men dedicatedly spotting train numbers while breathing in the diesel fumes. It can be train or plane numbers, stamps, toy soldiers, books, postcards, fossils or vinyl records, these men will collect anything.

What they collect is less significant than the act of accumulation. Not all these avid hobbyists are collectors. Some spend hours on the river bank or by the canal, fishing for the big one, although it's invariably a tiddler they go home with. Others go on long, lonesome hikes across moor and mountain, with only sheep for company. Whatever their obsession, these men have one thing in common – they are all Trainspotters.

Trainspotter is the archetypal male loner. He's insular, provincial and detached. He's not particularly articulate unless he's talking about his hobby – hobby may be too mild a description for what is, in fact, an all-consuming passion – and he has little interest in politics, current affairs, or, indeed, the opposite sex. He's strong on repetition, routine, minutiae, loyalty, perfection, precision and single-mindedness. He's weak on dynamism, charisma, risk, creative imagination and entrepreneurialism. Some Trainspotters apply their strengths to their work rather than to a hobby. They make excellent accountants, librarians and middle-ranking civil servants – any job requiring the sort of dulling routine and attention to detail that would mush the brains of Alpha Male, Murdoch and Achilles.

Although I've seen many Trainspotters over the years, I didn't realise how many were actually out there until women I was interviewing started to alert me to them. Women would recall in sheer amazement the number of men they'd met who seem to live their lives through a hobby. They just couldn't understand these men's devotion to stamps, fly-fishing, antique brass thingies. They were astounded that a man would, on hearing a rare bird had flown in from the continent, drive hundreds of miles, all through the night if necessary, just to see it. These women found it incredible, sad is more accurate, that grown men would prefer to spend their evenings playing with their extensive and impressive model railways rather than playing with them.

These mostly brief encounters with Trainspotters did nothing to encourage the women to think that men were coping very well with the twenty-first century. Up to a point, they were quite correct in that assessment – many men can't fathom this new era and Trainspotter is one of them. Different faces cope with this male crisis of confidence in different ways. What Trainspotter does is absorb himself totally and completely in something over which he's got an element of control and which is measurable – and if that compels him to sit on Euston railway station waiting for the 6.30 from Glasgow to arrive so he can spot its number, so be it.

What we have with Trainspotter is a very straightforward, simple kind of guy. He's no twenty-first century male, just the opposite – more early nineteenth century in fact. What he's doing is devoting himself to the creation of an alternative world, a masculine comfort zone to which he can retreat when the real world becomes too difficult to handle.

Can Trainspotter be trusted in love?

If after a series of bad experiences with Manchild, Romancer or Cool Poser, you now yearn for just one thing in a man – that he be trustworthy – go for Trainspotter. This male face will roam, but only as far as the next hobbies shop, canal side or moorland path. When he says he's off to Heathrow to spot the planes for the day, you can be sure he means it. You may not understand why he does it, and you'd no more think of joining him than you'd quit watching TV soaps, but you'll always know where he is, and you'll always know he'll come home, having caught only a cold.

Is Trainspotter romantic?

To be good in the romance stakes, you have to know and understand the object of your desire. Ideally, you should have some awareness of how men and women relate as actual or potential sexual partners. It helps immensely if you can be intimate with your loved one without having to concentrate too hard. None of these are Trainspotter's strengths. Put another way, your average Trainspotter has about as much understanding of the female mind as Donald Trump has of poverty. He knows it exists, it just doesn't figure too highly in his life.

The amazing thing is, few Trainspotters realise how women see them. The reason for this is that Trainspotters view the world, and other people, through their own narrow gaze. Imagination is not one of their strong points. Several women I interviewed told of coming across Trainspotters after placing ads in personal columns or on Internet dating sites. They could tell which men were Trainspotters because, if these men were replying to the woman's advert by leaving a phone message, they'd give their name, age, job, and then spend the rest of the message talking about their love of fishing or stamp collecting. One man even invited the woman recipient to join him on one of his trainspotting outings to York – not a good romantic overture to a woman he'd yet to meet.

Some of these Trainspotters seemed to approach romance and courtship in the same way they went about collecting toy soldiers. They'd decide what they thought they needed in a woman, and then set out to find someone who fitted those specific criteria. One woman had received an email from a potential Trainspotter suitor who had responded to her profile on an Internet dating site. The message was a complete ramble until the point came when he felt he had to broach the subject of what sort of woman he was looking for. Amazingly, he then listed his 'preferences in a woman' so that she could 'measure herself' against his criteria. No doubt he's still looking.

Is Trainspotter the marrying kind?

Trainspotters are true bachelors, unless they are captured by a particularly brave and resolute female while still in their early years. Up to their early thirties, Trainspotters are amenable to some change, but after thirty-five, forget it. So if you think you could cope with the particular lifestyle of Trainspotter, try to get him down the aisle before he's thirty. Once you have him, he'll follow you like a faithful hound – obedient, loyal, generally well-behaved and dutiful, but if you want him to lick you, you'll have to ask.

What sort of woman does Trainspotter go for?

The happiest Trainspotters are those who have a partner who will permit them the space to follow their chosen pastime, a wife who won't complain when her Trainspotter husband wants to spend loads of dosh converting the garage into storage space for his collection of Toby Jugs. Some Trainspotters do go for like-minded souls, women who are themselves only too happy sitting quietly, waiting for the large pike in the reeds to show itself, but there aren't many of them about these days. This is where love and romance mirror Trainspotter's patient character – he may have high aspirations, but invariably he has to settle for what happens to swim past on the day.

What is Trainspotter like as a father?

Not much use although to be fair, most Trainspotters fall into parenting by accident, any design originating from their wives. If you've married a Trainspotter and he's fathered your children, you know what to expect, and that won't be a househusband. You can, however, be sure he'll take his son along on his fishing, bird-watching or stamp collecting expeditions – junior and senior Trainspotters together, a perfect meeting of minds. If he has a daughter, unless she's willing to join them, and that's unlikely, she'll be with you all day.

Could you work for Trainspotter?

It's unlikely that you would work for this male face. He's more likely to be a colleague down on the shopfloor, in the general office or by the checkout. He's ambitious, but not for his job. Highlights of his life are spotting nesting ospreys at Bassenthwaite Lake in northern England, not usurping Alpha Male's throne.

Some Trainspotters do manage to transpose their hobby to their work by opening angling or hobby shops. If you work for him in one of these, you're likely to have a decent boss. Just make sure you're a Trainspotter as well, or the repetition will send you slightly crazy.

Would you like Trainspotter as a friend?

This face is one of the best of all friends, so long as you share his interest. If you don't twitch, spot or collect, have no worries, your paths are unlikely to cross, unless you are a jogger who's happened to trip over Trainspotter's extended fishing rod left lying across the canal tow path.

Scientifically speaking

French sociologist Jean-Francois Lyotard coined the term 'performativity' to describe a particular condition of the postmodern age. He argues that with the demise of religious and political 'grand-narratives', individuals increasingly rely on pseudo-scientific knowledge to give their lives meaning. More and more, we look to numbers, data, tables, indicators – so-called objective criteria that can be measured and thereby evaluated for their worth. This is what Trainspotter is doing. He is in pursuit of scientific measurement to give his life purpose and himself meaning. The train or plane number, size of fish, species of birds, types of stamps, can all be logged, catalogued, 'scientifically' evaluated and measured. This is how he engages with the world and, importantly, tries to manage it.

Is Trainspotter the man for you

Trainspotter is a traditionalist through and through – steady, dependable, likeable even, but rather boring. He loves the routine and regularity of domestic life, but can be infuriating to live with, being rather anally retentive in his habits. He is extremely tidy and obsessed with detail. So if you are the sort of woman who tends to fling her dirty undies and stockings under the bed, leave the washing-up until the weekend, and rely on the bank to pay your bills, Trainspotter sounds the perfect counterbalance to your inherent chaos – or he may drive you completely mad.

If sex is important to you, know that most Trainspotters approach lovemaking in their particular inimitable style – typically, missionary position, in the dark, and on alternate weekends. If you love to dance naked under a full moon, are into spanking or group sex, Trainspotter would definitely be a challenge. He might just let you get on with it while he heads for the peace and quiet of the river bank.

If you do decide to sample Trainspotter, be aware that it's often difficult to tell his true age. At twenty-five he can look ready for retirement, yet at sixty-five he looks, well, sixty-five. For Trainspotter, youth was merely a necessary phase before he reached his true life stage – middle age.

To sum up

Although born into the second half of the twentieth century, Trainspotter has never really come to terms with the modern era. Like Zebedee, he finds it all a bit too confusing and complicated. Alpha Females, new-age culture, dope fiends, sexual crossing – he may have a sense of what such terms mean, but don't expect him to come to the party. Sure, he gets his kicks, but down on the station platform, in the coin shop, not in the bedroom. Often I've reflected on whether Trainspotters are always condemned to watch, never participate. Do they not feel the tiniest bit envious of the suntanned hordes flying home from Tenerife? Is their compulsion constantly to replay the battle of Waterloo with toy soldiers an indicator that, at heart, Trainspotters are frustrated Napoleons or Wellingtons? Is the model railway in the converted attic no more than an entirely understandable desire to recreate the romantic age of steam? Or are they just little boys who've never quite grown up?

It's easy to be a little harsh on Trainspotter, but isn't there something endearing about his boyishness, his innocence in the face of the modern world? Okay, he's fixated, but before you dismiss him completely, just reflect on the depth of love this man has in his heart, for only a deep love could compel him to cram his home with the object of his desire, to spend every spare hour searching for it, or to fill countless little black books with its details. Just be thankful he's not like that with women. If he were, we'd name him Romancer.

HOW TO SPOT A TRAINSPOTTER

Look for someone in weather-proof clothing, heading off for Gatwick, King's Cross or the upper reaches of the Thames.

HOW DOES TRAINSPOTTER PERFORM IN THE BEDROOM?

Bet he records every sticky moment in a little red book. Thing is, how long will it take to fill it?

WHAT IF TRAINSPOTTER IS YOUR PARTNER?

As by now you'll have realised, you've caught one of the most faithful yet obstinate of all the male faces. But what do you do now you've got him?

MOST LIKELY TO SAY

'Has my copy of *Angling Today* arrived yet?'

KEY QUESTION

If you want him to fall in love with you, where do you choose for your first romantic weekend away – York with its world-famous railway museum, Paris in the spring, or Ibiza?
Answer: Take him to Paris – it has the famous Metro. He's already been to York countless times, while Ibiza has no railway.

Uniform Man

Main characteristics

Sees himself as a warrior male; emotionally insecure; a follower not a leader; one of the lads; rigid but brittle temperament.

What's he like?

Most males go through a period in their lives when they want to be soldiers, firemen, policemen or in the SAS. All that masculine action, bravado and gung-ho is irresistible to male minds, especially younger ones. Just how compelling is apparent in the number of television programmes that feature 'strong men' in 'action', stories about detectives, special forces, secret agents. Indeed, if we didn't have men in uniform to act out their adventures for us, there'd be even less on TV or at the cinema than there is already. The vast majority of males eventually grow out of their desire to be in Delta Force or leading a SWOT team. Instead, they end up being Corporate Man, Libman or even Wallflower – but not all of them. A few do become the real thing, and in so doing they come to live out a particular dimension of the masculine dream. They are Uniform Men.

Uniform Man exists as a stereotype, which is a problem. Once he's officially enlisted, Uniform Man is straightaway under a lot of pressure to perform one of the most dominant types of masculinity – invariably highly macho, aggressive and loud, marginalises women, especially as workmates, and usually has a strong undercurrent of homophobia about it. The most obvious place to see such masculinity in action is in the armed forces, but it is also evident in the police and fire services, and even among street gangs and criminal groups. Just how powerful these male messages are for Uniform Man was revealed in a recent incident in America where a Mafia boss was rubbed out for being gay.

Uniform Man has a lot in common with Rottweiler, Neanderthal and Club Man – all four are heavily into male bonding, brotherhoods and fraternities. They get their kicks from being with like-minded men, but don't dare question these guys' sexuality. The fact that many of them have gay or bi leanings remains one of the darker secrets of the lads' locker-room. The main difference with Uniform Man is that, through his training, he's a very disciplined and skilled bloke. He can walk through fire, survive for weeks in the jungle, kill with his bare hands, even take out Saddam Hussein given half a chance. He actually lives out, in a very real and sometimes deadly and dangerous way, the death and glory imagery that throughout history has surrounded all men in uniform.

Given the attraction that uniforms seem to have for the male mind, it's not surprising that there are many wannabe Uniform Men around – guys who haven't quite got there but would like to. You'll see wannabe Uniform Man with his mates in town at the weekend, lads all wearing the same gear, on the prowl, not unlike a wolf pack pursuing its prey. It's not just the uniform that attracts these weekend warriors; it's a chance to bond with other men – a fraternity of 'good blokes', chasing skirt together, getting pissed together, being idiots together. Many team sports, such as football, rugby and basketball, have this brotherhood mentality. In fact, you often find team managers deliberately trying to establish it as a way of ensuring the team pulls together. Wearing the uniform is more than just an indication of Uniform Man's affiliations. It gives him a strong sense of confidence and self-esteem – it tells him he's a man's man.

Can Uniform Man be trusted in love?

The answer to this question is, it depends. What it depends on is the extent to which he feels he can get away with a bit on the side without you knowing. Many of the male faces will succumb to temptation if they think they won't be found out, and Uniform Man is no different. What is different about him is that he can be controlled, but first he needs a wife or partner who sets down very strong and clear rules about his behaviour. Don't ever try this with Alpha Male or Murdoch, but you can with Uniform Man. He loves boundaries, directives, regulations. He likes to know his limits, especially in the game of love.

The saddest Uniform Men are those who live alone, without male or female company, just drifting. They don't have the inner resources of more nomadic faces, such as Backpacker, and they're usually lacking the social sophistication and intellectual qualities of Achilles or Libman. Most Uniform Men are bright enough to recognise they'd be no good as bachelors, which is why they always like to come home to a loved one. But that fear of losing you won't stop Uniform Man shagging away if he thinks you won't mind, or won't notice. Of course, you'll do both, so don't give him the chance. Keep this male face on a fairly tight rein.

Is Uniform Man romantic?

Despite his outward posturing and swagger, Uniform Man is quite brittle – strong up to a point and then he can snap. This is especially so in the game of love and romance. He derives his strength from his mates, less so from the woman in his life, whom he will nevertheless love in a very traditional way. So while Uniform Man will outwardly be very confident and assured parachuting into enemy territory, when it comes to romance he can be a complete mess, very confused and uncertain. He spends so much time with his mates he's never really learned to relate to the female mind. Consequently, deep down he's afraid of women. Like Club Man, he's fearful of rejection and of his own sexual and emotional inadequacies. So don't expect too much in the way of romance from this male face. In fact, the very idea of being romantic is likely to embarrass him, make him feel uneasy. He'd love to say or write words of passion to his beloved, but he lacks the confidence. All the while there's that nagging question in his mind – what would my mates think if they knew I'd spent two hours, and a lot of money, buying twenty-four red Baccarat roses for my girlfriend? But even if he got as far as buying them, do you think he'd walk down the high street with the bouquet in his hand, to deliver them personally? You must be joking.

Is Uniform Man the marrying kind?

Yes, no doubt about that. He's up for marriage, the whole works, which is nice for you if you're the marrying type yourself. Just imagine the wedding scene. Coming out of a delightful rural church, arm in arm with your Uniform(ed) Man, him with a chest full of medals, you with your Thai orchids, there would be a ten-man saluting party of fellow Uniform(ed) Men, a tunnel of gleaming swords raised to the sun for you both to walk beneath. That would be an unforgettable picture to hand down to your grandchildren.

What sort of woman does Uniform Man go for?

If he's out for a quick fumble in the bushes, Uniform Man will go for whatever is available. If he's after a longer relationship, he's likely to be most attracted to a woman who is happy to play housewife. The majority of Uniform Men live very strange lives – they can be on call all hours of the day and night, they often have to manage on little sleep and snatched meals, and be prepared to put their lives on the line at a moment's notice. These are not the best conditions for a contented, quiet, domestic existence, which is precisely why Uniform Man is happiest when there is a dutiful wife back home, keeping the kitchen clean, the kids happy, the cat fed and the bills paid. He needs a wife or partner to keep it all together, to be his rock, his emotional anchor. Having all this at home spurs him on to fight enemies and danger at home and abroad – he convinces himself he's in Afghanistan for the sake of his family. Don't believe it – single and childless men are there, too.

What is Uniform Man like as a father?

Much as he will love and cherish his children, this face is not at his best as a dad. He can be something of a disciplinarian or can go to the other extreme, leaving it all to his wife to sort out. While he might make an excellent drill sergeant for a cohort of weedy young recruits, the self-confidence of Uniform Man tends to come undone when faced with toddler tantrums.

Could you work for Uniform Man?

If you do find yourself working for this male face he'll probably treat you in a very commanding fashion – with clear instructions, underlying discipline, rules and regulations, and penalties if you step out of line. However, the fact that Uniform Man is more likely to be a follower of other men than a leader tells us that he's unlikely to be exercising power on the board of directors. He may well make it to sergeant or petty officer level, but his mentality is straitjacketed to think in terms of hierarchies, with him not at the top. Uniform Man's not threatened by this; on the contrary, he respects the boss, the Alpha Male. As he sees it, without a hierarchy, the team cannot function. So don't go looking for Uniform Man in a Rolls, unless he's the chauffeur or bodyguard.

Would you like Uniform Man as a friend?

Friendship is a big thing for Uniform Man. He's not a loner as are Murdoch or Backpacker. He needs men around him because they signal to him how to think and behave. Uniform Man's biggest fear is being cast out, excluded, exiled from the group, identified as different, because that is all too threatening. In fact, the saddest Uniform Men are those who are 'let go' by their employers – they often end up having a real emotional crisis as a result. Uniform Man's greatest wish is to be accepted by his mates, and ideally looked up to as a strong man. When Uniform Man has achieved this accolade, he is in heaven.

Scientifically speaking

Sociologist Erving Goffman wrote of 'total institutions', describing them as 'the forcing houses for changing persons; each is a natural experiment on what can be done to the self'. These usually male-dominated environments shape and mould men's identities to fit in with their overpowering culture, a physical and mental process that cannot be resisted by those who expose themselves to it. The pervasiveness of militaristic ideologies on the minds of impressionable men is not to be underestimated. This is the attraction for Uniform Man – to submit his identity to a powerful male culture in return for being verified as 'a man'.

Is Uniform Man the man for you?

If you are seeking a very traditional relationship with a bloke who sees himself as a bit of a man's man and who knows how to polish your shoes, you could do worse than this face. You'll have to be stronger than him emotionally – don't try to compete with the arm wrestling – and you must resist the temptation to scream at him when he tells you his Christmas leave has just been cancelled. Okay, complain a little but then get on with it – if you want domestic regularity, marry Teddy Bear.

Uniform Man is quite predictable, he won't want to go off to university to study philosophy as a mature student, and if he makes it up the ranks, he's likely to retire early on a decent pension. You will, however, have to keep an eye on him when the young blonde single mother moves in next door. He'll always return home from playing soldiers and detectives, but just when you'll never be quite sure. So if you are the sort of woman who wants to know what her bloke is up to at all times of the day and night, Uniform Man is not for you. He does, however, follow orders. You just have to make sure you give them to him very clearly.

Uniform Man sees himself as a warrior. Most women know that the real work is done at the nest site, not on the parade ground, but you cannot tell him this truth. You have to let the warrior return home and imagine himself as the head of the family, if only for as long as his leave lasts. This is one illusion you must maintain, and you must do it so his sense of masculinity is not compromised.

Finally, you should know that due to the types of jobs they do, many Uniform Men can easily succumb to what I term the 'SAS syndrome'. In other words, they convince themselves that they are members of an élite bunch of guys. One Uniform Man I came across used to tell anyone who'd listen that he'd been in the SAS, but he was just a squaddie at Catterick Camp. Uniform Men, whether detectives, firemen, sailors or camp cooks, live in a hyper-masculine world that draws a lot on male fantasies. It's a world that can turn quite nasty in an instant. So if you marry him, be aware that you are joining his regiment too. There is no escape from that. To many women he may sound a bit simple, but then again, uniforms can be so very sexy.

To sum up

This is one of the oldest types of male face. Ever since the males of the species first banded together out on the African savannah to hunt sabre-toothed tigers, there's been Uniform Men – brothers together, armed to the teeth and ready for anything. In those far-off days, and at regular intervals ever since, we've needed to rely on Uniform Man to save our homes, save our children, save our lives. We've gone to our Uniform Men to protect us – mostly from other Uniform Men.

HOW TO SPOT A UNIFORM MAN

Always carries some form of identification, even when not in uniform. Look for a man with tattoos and a badge.

HOW DOES UNIFORM MAN
PERFORM IN THE BEDROOM?

If he's not too stressed from his latest brush with death and evil, he should be okay. If he is on the edge, let him sleep it off or go for a long walk together – not a route march.

WHAT IF UNIFORM MAN IS YOUR PARTNER?

I have no doubt whatsoever that your infinite patience must have been sorely tested during this relationship, and so it will continue until the day dawns when he decides to pack up all this juvenile male bonding stuff and become Corporate Man.

MOST LIKELY TO SAY

'I've invited my mates along for the christening. Can you get some booze in?'

KEY QUESTION

If you are married to an aspiring, not a true, Uniform Man, how do you keep him happy and content with life?
Answer: Encourage him to join the Territorials. Every weekend or so he'll come home bruised and muddy, but at least he'll buy you flowers in appreciation of you washing his gear.

WALLFLOWER

Main characteristics

Unambitious couch potato; predictable behaviour patterns; passive and mostly docile; bit of a mummy's boy.

What's he like?

Many of the male faces can be said to show extremes of personality – there is usually something you can find attractive in them as well as something that makes you want to stay away. This is not the case with Wallflower. He's your archetypal ordinary bloke, a middling sort of guy with little to mark him out as different or special. If you imagine the world of men as some sort of army, Murdoch would be Napoleon, Alpha Male and Achilles the generals and political leaders, Uniform Man and Rottweiler the sergeants and NCOs, and in the infantry, footslogging behind, would be lots of Wallflowers.

Wallflower derives his name from the fact that he's a man who stays in the background and makes up the numbers. He rarely ventures a strong opinion, unless it's about a favourite subject of his – typically, booze, sport, women or cars. He has a tendency to agree with whatever stronger-minded males say, and he'd most likely walk away from emotional or physical confrontation. Wallflower is one of life's laid-back watchers. He's not a doer. This is no action man we have here. He is a follower, not a leader. He loves comfort, security, routine and predictability. What he hates is change.

Wallflower is one of the more balanced faces. He's especially good at balancing on fences, and when that position becomes too uncomfortable, he'll go to the fridge, pour himself a cold lager and head for the couch. He has an amazing capacity to slouch there for hours, ruminating on life's little quandaries, of which he has little understanding, and otherwise contentedly absorbed in Sky Sport or *Coronation Street*. When he does surface it will be to go to the loo or to get more lager. His other talent is an ability to block out difficult, he would say 'mindless', problems, examples being global warming, famine in Africa, threats to world peace and the latest Middle East crisis. If Preacher is standing on a soapbox in Hyde Park, haranguing one man and his dog, Wallflower will stop and listen for a few minutes, agree with everything he said, and then head off to the nearest pub.

Wallflower is self-evidently no adventurer or trailblazer. He wouldn't have been leading the Charge of the Light Brigade; he wouldn't have signed up for the Mayflower as it prepared to set sail for the New World; and he's unlikely ever to set foot on the moon. He's never invented anything, painted a masterpiece or designed a postmodern museum. He's happy merely to chug along on half-power, do his job and get his knowledge of the world from tabloids and television.

You might think to yourself, 'I don't think I've ever met a Wallflower.' Let me assure you, you have; you found them so invisible you didn't register them. They were there, but not there – present but absent. You are much more likely to have met many Wallflowers than none. Some women I talked to were convinced that this male face was the most common of all. Several of them had been married to one. Note the past tense.

Wallflowers are not inherently unlikeable, but they can be a little infuriating to those male and female faces who are altogether more dynamic and go-getting. Wallflower's desire for a quiet life is understandable up to a point – who wants to be permanently stressed out? – but to wrap yourself around in a comfort blanket of television, sport and drink is rather sad really. But then, perhaps we need Wallflowers so that Alpha Males and Corporate Men have someone they can boss around.

Can Wallflower be trusted in love?

Like several of the male faces, Wallflower will not say no to a clear 'come on' from the brunette down at the off-licence. However, shagging around is really not for him. Adultery requires quite a bit of mental, and physical, energy. You have to plan, prepare, calculate, evaluate, protect and act if you want to be chasing a bit of the other – ask Romancer. None of these attributes are to be found in Wallflower. Sure, he might like to think of himself as a bit of a ladies' man, but so do most blokes. The reality is that, again like most men, Wallflower gets sex when he stumbles across it quite by chance, is married, or does it himself.

He'll go looking for a little carnal pleasure now and again, he's quite normal in that way, but he's unlikely to find it. It might, on occasion, find him. If you are living with a Wallflower, once a week should be more than enough to keep him at home. Any more and he's likely to retreat to his rest home – the couch. Any less and he'll start flicking through the porno channel on the TV.

Is Wallflower romantic?

This is another of those male faces who needs educating in the ways of love and romance. Buy him a self-help book, nothing too deep and something that you can 'innocently' leave lying around the home to catch his eye. He'd never, ever buy such a book himself, but once he's started reading it he'll quite enjoy it. In fact, if he manages to read to the end, he'll have learnt that much he'll see himself as quite a switched on 'modern man'. He's never going to be able to compete with the likes of Achilles, Jeffrey or even Cool Poser when it comes to playing the game of love and romance, but over time he can come to feel less inadequate.

If you are in love with a Wallflower it's important to go easy with him, especially at first. If you are too pushy or demanding, you'll frighten him off. Suddenly, he won't be phoning you, he won't be answering your calls, he'll be starting to back off, probably to the sofa or the pub. Remember his natural place is following behind, and this doesn't just mean his boss at work. It means his boss at home, too – and that will be you if you set up home with him. With patience, you'll have him just where you want him. He can be trained to remember certain important events such as your birthday, your wedding anniversary, the day you first met. So long as you operate a mix of reward and punishment, he'll remember the flowers and chocolates on these special occasions. Don't expect anything spontaneous – Wallflower doesn't do spontaneity.

Is Wallflower the marrying kind?

The real question is, are you the marrying kind for Wallflower? Sure, he'll get married, but often for all the wrong reasons – you've told him to and he's too scared to say no; he's left his mum and now desperately seeks a mum-wife; you earn more than him and he wants a new car; he can't find unprotected sex anywhere else; or he fancies the honeymoon in Florida.

As a male face, Wallflower is pretty easy to suss out. Much

more important is who you are. Don't go down the aisle with this guy unless you're totally confident you want him for the duration – or at least the next few years.

What sort of woman does Wallflower go for?

Like Rottweiler, when it comes to women Wallflower tends to get picked rather than do the choosing. His approach to relationships tends to mirror his attitude to life generally – he sits around and waits for it to happen to him, he doesn't go out and grab a slice of it for himself. If pushed to choose, he'd go for a woman who can keep him in the manner to which he is accustomed – featherbedded and comfortable.

What is Wallflower like as a father?

Wallflower and fatherhood are a peculiar mix. When you tell him you're pregnant he won't quite believe that he's managed to do it. In fact, he'll be tempted to think it's all down to you, until you remind him of his part in the process. However, as the great day gets closer, his pride will be replaced by nervousness, although he'll attempt to hide his anxieties by being nonchalant and blasé, especially in front of his mates. Don't bother having him at your bedside on the day – he'll be pretty hopeless. Let him come in when it's all over, pick up the sleeping bundle and play proud dad for a minute or two. The first few years will be traumatic for everyone and it's at this stage that Wallflower shows his real self – his lethargy. Don't expect him to bottle feed baby at night, or volunteer for nappy changing duty. You may occasionally get him to push the pram. By the time your brood are teenagers, Wallflower will be a middle-aged dad and well rooted to the couch and TV. He'll love you and his kids, but if you had a pound for every row you two had about his role as a father you'd be able to retire, kids and all, to Bermuda.

Could you work for Wallflower?

Most leaders need to be determined and more than a little obsessed with success. Wallflower is neither. As one woman who knew a Wallflower said to me, 'The reason they haven't joined the rat-race is because they don't want to. This type of guy does an office job because he needs the money, but would much prefer to see his wife or girlfriend go up the career ladder than himself.' This is a pretty accurate appraisal of Wallflower. They make excellent department store salesmen, not heads of corporations. If they do have a vocational talent, it's usually well hidden. On the plus side, his total lack of ambition means that Wallflower is one of the easiest male faces to work with. There's none of the political game playing you get with Chameleman or Achilles.

Would you like Wallflower as a friend?

The Wallflowers I have known have had several good qualities for friendship. They are amicable, mostly even-tempered, generally loyal, can be good listeners and quite easygoing. Their humour tends to be sardonic, which admittedly is not to everyone's taste, but a little bit of acerbic wit from the couch potato can work wonders at times, especially when used to deflate the egos of more pompous male faces.

Scientifically speaking

Wallflower is a particularly interesting face to examine within the sociology of masculinity for he appears to disavow what feminists such as Lynne Segal identify as the 'macho solidarity of the culture of work'. Work for most adult males provides an environment in which to develop their distinctly male personalities. By contrast, Wallflower prefers to remain snuggled up in the comfort blanket of the private sphere, the world of domesticity, the realm of the matriarch. By so doing, Wallflower is not rejecting the possibility of exercising male power; rather he's exercising power through inactivity, thereby placing the responsibility for his continued existence where it's always been – with his mother and, subsequently, his wife.

Is Wallflower the man for you?

With Wallflower you risk getting into bed, physically and metaphorically, with a 'mummy's boy' – a bloke who is reluctant to leave the milky warm bosom of the home hearth. As one woman said to me, 'There are a lot of mummy's boys out there. When my girlfriends and I are out we can easily spot them – they look rather innocent really, not sure how to cope with adult women. We do have a laugh at them, though some are quite nice.'

'Nice' is a good word to describe Wallflower. He doesn't have the aggressive edge of Rottweiler; he won't burst a blood vessel like Mr Angry will; he won't run off like Backpacker most certainly will; and he isn't intent on changing the world, as Preacher is. So go for Wallflower if you want a quiet life, are happy to be the breadwinner as well as mum to him and the kids, and you prefer a male face you can manage rather than one who'll try to manage you. You'll have problems getting him excited about anything very much, but you'll always know precisely where he is on his days off – on the couch.

To sum up

Compared to some other male faces, Wallflower is one of your gentler guys. He's neither obsessive nor aggressive. However, he does have a downside and that's his laziness. He is inherently lethargic, preferring others to lead while he follows. He'd much prefer the woman to take charge of his life than have to do it himself. The reason he hasn't joined the rat-race is simply because he doesn't want to get a sweat on. He'll work for a living, but only because he needs the money. Completely lacking in ambition, Wallflower will always be the last to get out of bed in the morning, but when he does, he'll make you breakfast if you tell him to.

HOW TO SPOT A WALLFLOWER

If unsure whether your date is a Wallflower or not, get him to talk about his favourite TV programmes. From that point onwards, the typical Wallflower will chat for hours.

HOW DOES WALLFLOWER
PERFORM IN THE BEDROOM?

Many Wallflowers are inherently shy, preferring to stay in the background rather than put their heads over the parapet, so don't expect fireworks. If you train him properly, you might get there eventually, but you can rule out swinging parties for sure.

WHAT IF WALLFLOWER IS YOUR PARTNER?

Have you heard of the division of labour? No, well that's because there isn't any in your house. You do it all.

MOST LIKELY TO SAY

'Let's not get into an argument over this.'

KEY QUESTION

Do you want a man you can control and boss around?

Answer: Only if you get turned on by wearing the trousers.

WAYNE

Main characteristics

The heroic man; unchanging, loyal and steadfast; an endangered male; holds on to traditional values.

What's he like?

For a large part of the twentieth century the Hollywood actor John Wayne epitomised a rugged type of heavy duty masculinity. He was the all-male hero, the friendly tough guy, the gentleman warrior. Whether Wayne was fighting Red Indians, defending the Alamo, leading the US Marines or rescuing a damsel in distress, he did his duty as a man. Wayne symbolised a sort of hyper-masculinity, a man who was quick with his fists, somewhat slower with his tongue, especially with the ladies, but who, through his doggedness, loyalty and personal honour, always won the day.

John Wayne didn't invent his screen character's maleness. It was already out there for him to come along and portray. Millions of people worldwide empathised with the sort of masculinity displayed by JW the actor, which is the main reason he was so successful. JW may have gone to the big ranch in the sky, but there are still many men for whom his type of maleness is the one with which they are most comfortable. These twenty-first century Waynes may not have consciously modelled themselves on their namesake, but they follow, to some degree, his chivalrous attitude towards women, his general moral fortitude, and his belief in doing what a 'man's gotta do', regardless of the personal cost. Unfortunately, while such attitudes were okay a few decades ago, they can be a real problem for latter-day Waynes.

One of the interesting aspects of masculinities is how they change over time. They go in and out of fashion. Alas, modern-day Wayne is a victim of this. His type of masculinity is not so popular today as it was in the 1940s or 1950s. Back then, audiences had little trouble recognising JW's maleness and applauding it. That was how men were supposed to behave. Today we have much more variety among men. Wayne is one of twenty-seven faces and the result is that his type of masculinity is on the decline, still around but under a lot of pressure. The world tends to be more cynical and untrusting than it was fifty years ago, a more knowing, sophisticated, yet complex place. There just isn't room for a simplistic, upstanding male face such as Wayne. He may still be liked, even admired, but secretly people see him as old-fashioned and just too gentlemanly. Wayne may be steadfast, but the world has moved on.

Can Wayne be trusted in love?

Never ask a Wayne this type of question. He will see it as a real insult to his masculinity. His male pride will be hurt, he will be affronted that you ever had the cheek to question his honesty, his faithfulness, his loyalty to his wife/partner/girlfriend. If you want a man you can trust, go for Wayne. If Romancer is at one end of the male spectrum, Wayne is at the other.

Is Wayne romantic?

This depends on what you consider to be romantic. If you are one of those women who loves traditional romance, with your guy always making the first move, always paying, rarely asking just doing, with you following on behind, dutifully and gracefully, then Wayne is for you.

Wayne puts his woman on a pedestal and there you will sit for the rest of your life. Even if you upped and left him he'd still forgive you. He'd blame himself, not you. Wayne loves with great passion. He is a one-woman man. He doesn't really understand modern woman, so he's very vulnerable here, but if he meets his soulmate, and that is you, be sure that you have a man who will shower you with all he has. He will worship you. The question is, can you handle being worshipped?

Is Wayne the marrying kind?

Wayne was made for marriage. He's no singleton, no mummy's boy, and nor is he a predatory male, sniffing out multiple lovers. Waynes are more likely to be the ones let down in love. They can find themselves darning their own socks, scanning the lonely hearts columns, sleeping alone, especially if they've got themselves involved with one of the naughtier female types. Wayne is never happy if forced to play such a bachelor boy role. For Wayne, being alone in a bedsit is not his preferred state of being. He's much better with a loving, faithful woman by his side. Wayne's approach to love and romance means that he sees heterosexual coupledom as the mainstay of society. He sees himself as a mainstay as well. Marriage fits perfectly with his conservative outlook on life.

If you come across a single Wayne, you'll quickly get the sense that this man is searching for something, someone. He may well appear a bit of a loner, insular, socially insecure, but all that will change once he falls in love. Remember, this is one of the most traditionally minded of all male faces. He sees himself as a man's man, but not in the same way that Uniform Man, Rottweiler or Neanderthal do. He may have such faces among his circle of friends, but for Wayne they are just part of the variety around him. They are not the types he wants to be. He really likes women. In fact, he respects them much more than he respects himself. What Wayne wants is to be with his male pals occasionally, but always to go home to his real love, his wife and family.

What sort of woman does Wayne go for?

As might be evident, Wayne is very vulnerable around women. His simplistic, rose-coloured view of the female species means that he can get dumped on at times. He doesn't realise that there are as many faces of women as there are of men, and not all of them are as sweet as apple pie. If he's lucky, he'll meet a steady, reliable, faithful, honest, homemaker type of woman when in his late teens or early twenties, and thereafter settle down to married bliss. If he's not so lucky, he'll meet vampgirl – a woman he'll adore, but who will lead him a merry dance. She'll not want to let him go, mainly because she knows there's too few guys like him around these days, but despite wanting to keep him she'll get bored by Wayne's niceness. After a while, she'll be seeing the naughty boys, Manchild, Romancer or Cool Poser. When Wayne finds out, he may be strong enough to wave her goodbye, but if not, he's in for a very steep learning curve downwards, at the end of which he'll hit rock bottom. Unfortunately, due to Wayne's lack of reflective emotional intelligence, he'll convince himself it was all his fault and thereafter carry a flame for the vixen who broke his heart. If you come across Wayne when he's toting such baggage and you want to nurse him, sponge his brow, bring him back into the sunshine through your love, you've got your work cut out. You'll get there in the end, but remember, while most of us are vulnerable after having lost in love, Wayne is one of the most exposed in such situations. In time, however, he'll take his ex-sweetheart off the pedestal – and replace her with you.

What is Wayne like as a father?

In Wayne's ideal world he'd be happily married with several children, at least one of whom would be a girl. Sons can be a little tricky for Wayne because he'll have high expectations of them as males simply because he sees them as coming from 'his male loins'. While this may be true biologically, in terms of masculine identity male sperm counts for zilch. His sons could turn out to be any of the male faces. As I said, Wayne is rapidly becoming one of the least common, which may be a pity but it's a fact, so it's much more likely his sons will turn out to be Cool Posers, Chamelemen or even Riskers. If that does happen, expect plenty of fireworks between Wayne and his male off-spring, especially during their teenage years.

As far as his relationship with his daughter is concerned, Wayne is much more comfortable. This would be the most important woman in his life, after you, naturally. Wayne would be able to play the role he's always wanted – that of the 'Big Man' at home, the patriarch protecting his family, and central to this self-image will be his daughter. She'll undoubtedly come to relish the love and attention he'll give her. 'Nothing is too good for my girl' will be his motto. However, things can go badly amiss when she starts to feel those pangs of juvenile sexuality and she yearns for a younger man who can love her in a different way from her dad. At this point, Wayne may become jealous, or even outright hostile if he feels his 'little girl' is involved with a 'bad 'un'. Let him go through this period. It's part of his education. Okay, it's come a little late in Wayne's life, but it's never too soon to see the world as it really is.

Could you work for Wayne?

This is one of the better male faces to work for. He's loyal, frank and usually honest. He's not the sort of guy to change careers much. He prefers to stay with the same job for many years. If you find yourself working for Wayne, you'll have to work as hard as he does, but he's likely to protect you from too much organisational hassle if he can.

Would you like Wayne as a friend?

Yes, he's one of the best. On a friendship level, Wayne is better with men than women, although he'd hate to admit it. He's the sort of guy you can ask favours of and he won't score them up against you for future use. He's very genuine, not particularly imaginative or insightful, but solid and dependable in most situations. If you are female and in a crisis, Wayne will delight in riding to your rescue, just like Big John.

Scientifically speaking

As American pro-feminist writer Michael Kimmel points out, 'Masculinism is, at its centre, resistance to femininity, to the forces that turn hard men into soft, enervated nerds.' Masculinists such as Wayne retreat to a patriarchal form of masculinity largely because they are 'terrified' of having their manhood challenged. As Kimmel's research shows, men retreating from mythical ideas of 'feminisation' are not new. Such ideas have a long history. However, Wayne is proof that the myth still holds sway with many men. Wayne may want to rescue women, but only so that he can reinforce his own identity as a man.

Is Wayne the man for you?

What you have with Wayne is a very endearing but rather prudish male, a guy who sees himself as very straight, sexually and in every other way, and who views the world in simplistic black and white terms. He doesn't like complexity, which is one reason why he feels safest when he's surrounded by structure and permanence – wife, kids and regular job.

If he takes your fancy, your relationship with Wayne will work best if you let him have this structure, but remember that Wayne's masculinity needs to be bolstered up now and again. He's in his element when putting something right for a female in need. In reality, this may mean fixing a shelf in the kitchen or paying your hairdressing bills, but in his imagination, he is much more than a man-about-the-house. He is a stalwart, a safe haven in a troubled sea. Wayne is one of the few male faces who still feels that he should be the main breadwinner in the family. He's not best suited to sitting in the background and playing second fiddle to an Alpha Female or becoming a househusband. He's hopeless at retirement and in crisis if he gets made redundant. He still thinks the man's role is to provide and protect, so unless you're prepared to go along with this view, you could have problems.

For Wayne, women occupy a certain place in the world – on a pedestal. If you'd like to be up there, great, but few women find that spot comfortable for long. Most want to be loved for their strengths and their weaknesses. If Wayne senses this, he can get very frustrated. He can't understand what he's doing wrong. He'd really like the chance to demonstrate his love for women by saving them, but unfortunately his suburban lifestyle provides him with few opportunities for this, so he resorts to being paternalistic, maybe a little patronising at times. He can be quiet and reserved around women, but occasionally act quite macho if he feels threatened. He's very traditional. He'll always open the door for a woman, but never put down the toilet seat after using it.

The twenty-first century is a difficult time for Wayne. He likes women, loves them even, but doesn't really understand them. He's a completely unreconstituted male, a man from the past, a guy who has modelled himself, at least subconsciously, around a very traditional, upright type of masculinity. Like his namesake, he belongs to another era. So if you prefer a good old-fashioned, stand-up type of guy, a 'big man', someone who is honest, conservative and unchanging, Wayne has to be your first choice.

To sum up

What we have with Wayne is a man who could be on the way out, unless the fashion in masculinity changes back to what it was fifty or more years ago. Despite being an endangered species, Wayne fervently believes his type of masculinity is the 'proper one'. If he ever has any inner doubts about that, he's just got to remember big JW, the man who won the West, the East, the North and the South as well as every battle he ever took part in, the hero who rescued countless women, and who always did 'what's right'. Unfortunately, the truth is that JW was an actor, his roles make-believe. His real name was Marion.

HOW TO SPOT A WAYNE

Look for a man who is always extremely courteous to women, but who gives the impression of not having yet caught up with the twenty-first century.

HOW DOES WAYNE PERFORM IN THE BEDROOM?

Should be a good rider.

WHAT IF WAYNE IS YOUR PARTNER?

There are not many like him left, so look after him. Keep him well serviced and he'll last for years.

MOST LIKELY TO SAY

'A man must do what a man must do.'

KEY QUESTION

Your daughter has decided she wants to go to university to do a degree in engineering, instead of what he hoped she'd do, which was teaching. Who tells him – you or your daughter? Or do neither of you tell him and just pretend she is studying leisure and tourism?

Answer: Tell him the truth and tell him together. It may hurt him initially but he'll come round.

ZEBEDEE

Main characteristics

Floundering and confused; needs nurturing; unreflective; busy bloke; blinkered and dizzy – needs to take time out.

What's he like?

One of the most popular British children's TV programmes of all time was *The Magic Roundabout*. It was about a bunch of puppets who, through the magic of the roundabout, went from adventure to adventure, always coming back to their roundabout home at the end of the day. A lot of adults used to watch the programme. It had a surreal quality while managing to remain comforting and warm.

One of the characters in the programme was an eccentric, bouncing figure called Zebedee. For me, Zebedee came to exemplify the pleasant confusion and chaos in the storyline. He was totally out of it, bobbing around, getting in the way, trying to contribute, turning up at the most unlikely times, and never sure of what he was about. Nobody really understood Zebedee, including probably himself. There is a man just like him, totally confused by virtually every aspect of the modern age, facing the world unsure of where he is, who he is or in what direction he is going. He lives in a hectic but limited and blinkered world, which he inhabits as if on a roundabout, going round and round to the point of distraction. Keeping busy is his way of avoiding difficult questions about his life.

This male face can be seen in many countries, many places. In France, recent research refers to middle-class Frenchmen being turned into 'miserable creatures who are intimidated by women in an increasingly matriarchal society'. In the UK, school-based research reveals 'a fearsome new breed of girl who rules the classroom, leaving sidelined males watching in awe'. In Japan, the rapid shift in gender roles is seen as 'damaging the psychological well-being of Japanese males'. Whether these studies are accurate or not, it's very clear something is happening and it's mainly happening to Zebedee.

Poor Zebedee is being left behind. He's a man in crisis, a male without a mission, a bloke adrift. Men like this are very sad creatures. Masculinity wasn't intended for analysis and counselling. It's meant to signify a guy ready for action, direction, strength, a man in control of his life. Men are supposed to know what they're about; they're supposed to be rational and purposeful. Zebedee would dearly love to be purposeful, he just doesn't know how.

I've come across quite a few Zebedees – confused men who have put up mental shutters so they don't have to gaze too long on what is, to them, an increasingly complex world. Zebedees have learnt how to close down, to pretend they're okay when they patently are not. They may laugh and smile like other blokes, but there is an undercurrent of unease and anxiety around them. They are not very good at self-evaluation and reflection, and tend to stumble from one crisis to another, usually blaming their predicaments on bad luck. Let me assure you, luck has nothing to do with it. This guy just cannot cope. Zebedee is falling into a gaping black hole. Are you the one to rescue him?

Can Zebedee be trusted in love?

As a result of feeling so impotent as a man, Zebedee is liable to drift into relationships almost by accident. He's not in control of the situation. He's allowing the situation, and other people, to control him. So while Zebedee is basically a trustworthy male face, if you were married to him you'd have to ensure that he didn't get hooked by a woman who felt sorry for him. It's not that he'd set out to be unfaithful – such scheming is beyond him – but he could allow himself to be trapped into an adulterous relationship by a streetwise woman.

Is Zebedee romantic?

Zebedee has several endearing qualities and being romantic is one of them. He isn't the sort of guy to do romance in a loud way, he's no Achilles or Jeffrey, but he's very good at just being simply loving and affectionate. This male face is not scared of intimacy and emotional display. In fact, he loves to be romantic. Just don't expect him to whisk you off to the South of France one weekend.

Zebedee is the sort of bloke who needs love and romance in his life. If it's not there he feels really empty. If you are his wife or partner, encourage him to send you little missives by email or text, and to phone you from work. Zebedee will be delighted to do this. It gives him a warm glow to feel you're not far from him, physically and emotionally. Romance is something that doesn't come easy to many of the male faces, but given the right encouragement, which he'll need, Zebedee can be a real Romeo.

Is Zebedee the marrying kind?

Unlike, say, Wayne or Sigmund, Zebedee doesn't need the structure of marriage to make him feel secure in a relationship. Most

Zebedees are really quite relaxed about marriage – if their partner wants it, okay, if not, that's fine as well. Don't mistake this attitude for indifference or take it as an indication that Zebedee is reluctant to commit to a relationship. If he's in love, he'll want commitment just as much as you do. Zebedee is a very trusting guy, so if you tell him you want to be his partner and for you both to live together for the rest of your lives, he'll accept that. Indeed, he'll be over the moon to have such love in his life, the reason being that the routine of a relationship makes Zebedee feel safe.

What sort of woman does Zebedee go for?

Younger Zebedees are likely to be still with mum into their thirties, having yet to acquire the courage to venture out from the nest. However, older Zebedees, when they get into heavy relationships, go for particular types of women, quite often ones who are not suitable for them at all. They are best mated with women who are steady, balanced but just a little spirited, women who are comfortable with the world they're in and don't see it as a dangerous place. In other words, women who are the complete opposite of Zebedee, astute enough to recognise him for what he is and love him all the more for it. However, what often happens is that Zebedees get involved with women who fancy them because they are quite open-faced men – innocent really. For some women, having a Zebedee is a little like adding to your collection of moths. He's not one of the rarest, nor one of the most common of male species, but you feel you should have one in your collection, otherwise it isn't quite complete. For female man-collectors, Zebedees are easy to spot, easy to catch and don't resist much. If poor Zebedee finds himself netted, he's had it. There's not much chance of him escaping unless his female keeper decides he's not worth the effort. Unfortunately for Zebedee, he really is little effort at all. So he often gets kept a long time – too long. This confinement only serves to make him more manic than he already was.

What is Zebedee like as a father?

If life is, for Zebedee, a succession of attempts to come to terms with the strange, the frightening and the bizarre, being a father can make it much worse for him. Parenthood can catapult Zebedees from one unpredictable existence straight into another – nappy rash, sleepless nights, the terrible twos and, later, the trauma of the teenager. So, much as he'll try to be a real hands-on dad, and often succeed, being a father is an experience from which Zebedees rarely emerge unscathed.

Could you work for Zebedee?

Zebedee is usually an honest, hard-working bloke, not very imaginative maybe, but nevertheless a reliable employee, and he often finds himself promoted to some sort of middle management job. When everyone above him has retired, resigned or got sacked, Zebedee is often all that remains. So up the ladder he goes. For a while, he'll be delighted and will buzz around like a wannabe Alpha Male. Then things start to go wrong, not at first because his sheer energy will plug the gaps, but in time the fraying at the edges will get worse until the whole thing unravels. He cannot delegate, lead or plan. He's too nice, too soft, and thinks Machiavelli is a new Arsenal signing. My advice to Alpha Males and Corporate Men – never promote a Zebedee above his natural level. Much as you might personally like the guy, don't be tempted to 'give him a chance' – he's absolutely hopeless as a boss.

Would you like Zebedee as a friend?

Zebedees are great to have as friends. Whether you are a woman or a man, Zebedee makes the perfect pal. You can invite him to any dinner party, soirée, luncheon or knees-up, safe in the knowledge that he'll be nice to everyone, won't get pissed and won't try to get off with your sister.

Scientifically speaking

One of the more recently explored concepts in psychoanalysis and sociology concerns the 'nomadic subject'. Giles Deleuze describes it as a non-unitary subjectivity, a fragmented and dis-located state of being and becoming in the world. Feminist writer Rosi Braidotti suggests that the nomadic individual is prone to 'zigzagging along', unaware of destination and often ignorant of environment. Zebedee is such a person. He is knot-ted up, always in transit, desperate to be stable and grounded, but never quite making it. Zebedee is not reconciled with him-self. He is caught in a postmodern, deconstructed world, his response to which is to retreat to the familiar, a pattern of behaviour he repeats endlessly.

Is Zebedee the man for you?

Married or not, Zebedees are not for the enlightened, indepen-dent-minded, strong-willed female – they'd crush him. It's not that Zebedee doesn't like women, he does. It's just that he has virtually no understanding of them. For Zebedees, modern woman is a strange, exotic species, not to be tampered with without protection. When he does fall in love, he is totally wrapped up in the emotion of it all and will be a very consider-ate and careful lover. This is when you see him at his best.

Bouncing around, energised by the love in his life, he can be good fun and a devoted companion, channelling his undoubted energy into the garden or DIY.

To sum up

Zebedee's limited capacity for standing still and looking at what is really going on around him means the familiar problems of his life and relationships keep coming back to haunt him. It never occurs to him to get off the roundabout and investigate this strange place – that would be altogether too threatening! As a result, many Zebedees feel totally ill-equipped to deal with the challenges of a changing world – better, and safer, to stay on the roundabout and watch it all as a revolving, if rather dizzy, spectator.

HOW TO SPOT A ZEBEDEE

Look for a man who is always very busy but doesn't seem to be going anywhere.

HOW DOES ZEBEDEE PERFORM IN THE BEDROOM?

The bedroom is the one place where Zebedee's phenomenal nervous energy can be used to good effect. First make sure there are plenty of mirrors, plenty of toys and the room's well sound-proofed.

WHAT IF ZEBEDEE IS YOUR PARTNER?

Well, that depends whether you are a man-collector or not. If you are, please let him go. If you keep him much longer, he's in danger of spinning out of it altogether. If you're not, I'm sure you've got used to keeping a maternal eye on him. Just so long as you've got a grip on reality, I guess it doesn't matter too much if he hasn't.

MOST LIKELY TO SAY

'What's going on?'

KEY QUESTION

Which birthday present most suits Zebedee – a fully paid up series of consultations with an alternative lifestyle guru, or a gift voucher for the local garden centre? Which one does he most need?

Answer: Tell him he can't have the second unless he takes up the first. He needs them both.

A FINAL WORD
ON MEN

Most books that purport to tell us about how men think tend to suggest they are a very different species from women. They talk a different language, have different brain types, or have very different aspirations. If that were ever true, it certainly isn't today. If this book hasn't convinced you of the variety among men, just look around you. Surely you can spot the different male faces among the men in your life. They are out there, probably not far from where you're sitting now.

My studies and research tell me that men aren't all the same any more than women are. Men don't all think alike, don't all speak the same language. They haven't even all got the same type of masculinity, thank goodness. Life would be really tedious if men were all alike. Fortunately, it's a much more complex world than we often appreciate. Sure, it's easy to stick men into one, two or even three boxes, but once we've done that, what are we left with? We're left with simplicity, not reality.

I hope that *The Many Faces of Men* has given you some insights into males that you didn't already have. At the very least it should tell you that men aren't necessarily all destined to be serial shaggers, power-hungry predators or mummy's boys. Men are a very mixed bunch, twenty-seven varieties in fact, and we can expect some new types to start emerging over the next decade or so. Fashions in masculinity are changing more rapidly than ever – just look at David Beckham.

So whether you are male or female, hetero or gay, it's worth keeping an eye on men. They're a fascinating species to study.